WORDPRESS

Table of Contents

CHAPTER 1: BASICS OF WORDPRESS

1.1 Blogging Technologies

The WordPress programming is an individual distributing framework that uses a PHPand-MySQL stage, which gives you all that you have to make your blog and distribute your substance powerfully without programing the pages yourself. To put it plainly, with this stage, all your substance is put away in a MySQL database in your facilitating account.

PHP (which represents PHP Hypertext Preprocessor) is a server-side scripting language for making dynamic Web pages. At the point when a guest opens a page worked in PHP, the server forms the PHP directions and after that sends the outcomes to the guest's program. MySQL is an open source social database the board framework (RDBMS) that utilizations Structured Query Language (SQL), the most famous language for including, getting to, and handling information in a database. In the event that that all sounds Greek to you, consider MySQL a major file organizer where all the substance on your blog is put away.

Each time a guest goes to your blog to peruse your substance, he makes a solicitation that is sent to your server. The PHP programming language gets that demand, acquires the mentioned data from the MySQL database, and afterward introduces the mentioned data to your guest through his Web program.

WordPress keeps up ordered and sorted documents of your distributing history consequently. This documenting procedure occurs with each post you distribute to your blog. WordPress utilizes PHP and MySQL innovation to sort out what you distribute with the goal that you and your perusers can get to the data by date, class, creator, tag, etc. When you distribute to your WordPress blog, you can document that post under any classification you indicate — a clever chronicling framework in which you and your perusers would then be able to discover posts in explicit classifications.

WordPress gives you a chance to make the same number of classes as you need for recording your blog entries. We've seen online journals that have only one classification and websites that have up to 1,800 classes — with regards to sorting out your substance, WordPress is about close to home inclination. Then again, utilizing WordPress classifications is your decision. You don't need to utilize the classification include on the off chance that you'd preferably not.

1.2 Interaction with Audience

An energizing part of blogging with WordPress is getting input from your perusers after you post to your blog. Input, or blog remarks, is much the same as having a guestbook on your blog. Individuals can leave notes for you that distribute to your site, and you can react and connect with your perusers in discussion. These notes can extend the musings and thoughts you present in your blog entry by allowing your perusers the chance to include their input's. On the WordPress Dashboard, you have full managerial power over who can leave remarks. Also, in the event that somebody leaves a remark with sketchy substance, you can alter the remark or erase it. You're additionally allowed to not permit remarks on your blog.

The blogging network says that a blog without remarks isn't a blog at all in light of the fact that trading sees with guests is a piece of what makes blogging famous. Permitting remarks on your blog welcomes your group of spectators individuals to include themselves in your talk. In any case, distributing a blog without remarks gives your perusers a chance to share of your distributed words latently and, at times, that is alright. For instance, if your substance on a disputable theme may pull in guest affronts, it is sensible to distribute a post without empowering the remark include. Generally, perusers see remarking as a fantastic encounter when they visit web journals since remarks make them part of the discourse. In any case, it's up to you.

RSS represents Really Simple Syndication. A RSS channel is a standard component that blog perusers have generally expected. So what is RSS, truly? RSS is kept in touch with the Web server in XML — Extensible Markup Language, as a little, smaller record that can be perused by RSS perusers. Think about a RSS channel as a syndicated, or distributable, auto-refreshing rundown of "What's going on" for your Web webpage.

By utilizing devices called feed perusers, perusers can download your feed consequently — that is, they can set their feed perusers to naturally find new content, (for example, posts and remarks) from your blog and download that substance for their utilization.

For blog perusers to keep awake to-date with the best in class content you post, they have to buy in to your

RSS channel. Most blogging stages permit RSS channels to be autodiscovered by the different channel perusers. The peruser needs just to enter your site's URL, and the program naturally finds your RSS channel.

The most ideal approach to comprehend trackbacks is to consider them remarks, aside from a certain something: Trackbacks are remarks left on your blog by different online journals, not individuals. Sounds impeccably sensible, isn't that right? All things considered, is there any good reason why inanimate wouldn't articles need to take an interest in your exchange?

All things considered, possibly it's not all that insane all things considered. A trackback happens when you make a post on your blog, and inside that post, you give a connect to a post made by another blogger on an alternate blog. When you distribute that post, your blog sends a kind of electronic notice to the blog you connected to. That blog gets the notice and posts an affirmation of receipt as a remark to the post that you connected to on their webpage. The data that is contained inside the trackback incorporates a connection back to the post on your site that contains the connection to theirs — alongside the date and time, just as a short selection of your post.

Trackbacks are shown inside the remarks area of the individual posts.

The update is sent by means of a system ping (a device used to test, or confirm, regardless of whether a connection is reachable over the Internet) from your website to the webpage you connect to. This procedure functions as long as the two sites support trackback convention. Practically all major blogging stages support the trackback convention. Sending a trackback to a blog is a pleasant method for telling the blogger that you like the data she displayed in her blog entry. Each blogger acknowledges trackbacks to their posts from different bloggers.

1.3 Handling Comment and Trackback Spam

The supreme worst thing about each blogger's presence is remark and trackback spam. At the point when online journals turned into the "It" things on the Internet, spammers saw a chance. In the event that you've at any point gotten spam in your email program, you comprehend what we mean. For bloggers, the idea is comparative and similarly as baffling.

Prior to online journals, you frequently observed spammers filling Internet guestbooks with their connections however not pertinent remarks. The explanation is straightforward: Web destinations get higher rankings in the real web search tools on the off chance that they have different connections rolling in from different locales. Enter blog programming with remark and trackback advances, and websites become prime rearing ground for many spammers.

Since remarks and trackbacks are distributed to your webpage openly and more often than not with a connect to the analyst's Web website — spammers got their website connections posted on a great many sites by making programs that naturally look for Web destinations with remarking frameworks and after that mallet those frameworks with huge amounts of remarks that contain connections back to their locales. No blogger preferences spam. Accordingly, blogging administrations, for example, WordPress, spend untold hours for the sake of leaving these spammers speechless, and generally, they're effective. Sometimes, be that as it may, spammers sneak through. Numerous spammers are hostile, and every one of them is inexplicable in light of the fact that they don't add to the discussions that happen in online journals.

1.4 WordPress as Content Management System

You hear it a ton in the event that you peruse diverse Web locales that distribute posts about WordPress: "WordPress is more than a blogging stage; it's a full content management system." What does that mean? A content management system (CMS) is a stage that gives you a chance to run a full Web website on your area. This implies WordPress, notwithstanding a blog, enables you to make pages and incorporate extra includes with your Web webpage that have nothing to do with the content on your blog. A Web website and a blog are two distinct things. Albeit a Web webpage can contain a blog, a blog can't contain a full Web website. We realize it sounds befuddling, yet after you read this segment and investigate the contrasts between the two, you'll have a superior comprehension.

A blog is a sequential presentation of content — regularly, composed by the blog creator. The posts are distributed and, normally, arranged into points and chronicled by date. Blog entries can have remarks actuated so readers can leave their input and the writer can react, making an exchange about the blog entry.

A Web webpage is a gathering of distributed pages and various segments that offer the guest an alternate encounter. A Web webpage can consolidate a blog however more often than not contains different segments and highlights.

1.5 Open Source and WordPress Licensing

Open source software will be software whose source code is uninhibitedly accessible to people in general and can be adjusted and redistributed by anybody without restriction or result. This is an exceptionally basic, watered-down form of the meaning of open source. Open source software source code must be uninhibitedly accessible, and any permitting of the open source software must comply with this definition. In light of the OSI definition, WordPress is an open source software venture. Its source code is open and freely accessible for anybody to see, expand on, and disseminate at no expense anyplace, at whenever, or in any capacity whatsoever.

Standard clients of WordPress software need never fret about the GPL of the WordPress venture by any means. Standard clients of the stage need to do nothing extraordinary to submit to the GPL. You don't need to pay to utilize the WordPress software, and you aren't required to recognize that you're utilizing the WordPress software on your site.

Most standard clients of WordPress aren't even mindful of the software authorizing in light of the fact that it doesn't influence the everyday business of blogging and distributing their destinations with the stage. Notwithstanding, it is anything but an impractical notion to instruct yourself on the rudiments of the GPL and attempt to be sure that any modules and subjects you use with your WordPress establishment submit to the GPL so you have significant serenity that all applications and software you're utilizing are in consistence.

The open authorizing that relates to WordPress modules and subjects wasn't chosen in an official courtroom. The present assessment of the best (lawful) rehearses is only that, sentiment.

WordPress modules and topics are derivative works of WordPress and, accordingly, must comply with the GPL by discharging the advancement works under a similar permit that WordPress has.

A derivative work, as it identifies with WordPress, is a work that contains programming whose usefulness relies upon the center WordPress records. Since modules and topics contain PHP programming that call WordPress center capacities, they depend on the center WordPress framework to work appropriately and, consequently, are augmentations of the software.

To keep up consistence with the GPL, module or topic designers can't discharge improvement work under any (prohibitive) permit other than the GPL. In any case, numerous module and subject designers have attempted to discharge material under different licenses, and some have been effective. Nonetheless, the WordPress people group by and large doesn't bolster these engineers and their modules and topics. Also, the center WordPress improvement group considers such works resistant with the permit, and consequently, the law.

1.6 WordPress Release Cycles

The open calendar for WordPress updates is, about, one new discharge at regular intervals. As a client, you can expect another arrival of the WordPress software around four times each year. We can validate that the WordPress advancement group adheres to that calendar intently, with exemptions just to a great extent. When they make special cases to the 120-day rule, they for the most part make an open declaration about it with the goal that clients realize what's in store and when to anticipate it.

For the most part, intrusions to the 120-day calendar happen in light of the fact that the improvement of WordPress is basically on a volunteer premise. A couple of designers — representatives of Automattic, the organization behind WordPress.com — are paid to create for WordPress, however most engineers are volunteers. In this way, the advancement of WordPress improvement relies upon the designers' calendars. When the most recent WordPress establishment ends up accessible, that form has experienced a few emphasess, or adaptations. This area causes you comprehend the stuff to get the most recent rendition to your Web webpage, and clarifies a portion of the WordPress improvement phrasing. After the WordPress advancement group issues a last discharge rendition, they start again in the alpha stage, equipping and getting ready to experience the improvement cycle for the following real form. Ordinarily, an improvement cycle keeps going 120 days. Be that as it may, this is a guess in light of the fact that any number of things can occur (from formative issues to troublesome bugs) to postpone the procedure.

In the event that you realize where to look, monitoring the WordPress improvement cycle is simple, particularly in light of the fact that the WordPress advancement group attempts to make the improvement procedure as straightforward as would be prudent. You can track refreshes by finding out about them in different spots on the Internet and by tuning in to discussions between designers. In case you're so disposed, you can bounce in and loan the engineers a hand, as well.

You have a few different ways to keep awake to-date on what's happening in the realm of WordPress improvement, including blog entries, live visits, advancement gatherings, following tickets, and bug reports, just to give some examples.

WordPress advancement moves quite quick. Regularly, changes in the WordPress software's improvement cycle happen day by day. While the engineers are working on alpha and beta forms and discharge up-and-comers, they will submit the most recent center changes to the storehouse and roll out those improvements accessible to the general population to download, introduce, and test without anyone else destinations. The progressions are discharged in a full WordPress software bundle called a daily form — which contains the most recent center changes submitted to the undertaking, changes that have not yet discharged as a full and last form, yet. Utilizing daily forms is anything but a protected practice for a live site. We unequivocally prescribe

making a test domain to test the daily forms.
Ordinarily, particularly during alpha and beta stages,
the center code may break and cause issues with your
current establishment, so utilize daily forms in a test
situation just and leave your live site unblemished
until the last discharge is accessible.

1.7 WordPress Community

Try not to give the sheer volume of clients a chance
to threaten you: WordPress has gloating rights to the
most supportive blogging network on the Web today.
A huge number of Web destinations exist that
spotlight everything from WordPress news, resources,
refreshes, instructional exercises, preparing — the
rundown is unending. Do a speedy Google scan for
WordPress and you'll get in any event 180,000,000
outcomes. Point is, WordPress clients are everywhere
throughout the Internet from Web destinations to talk
discussions and informal communities to web
recordings, and that's only the tip of the iceberg; and
for some individuals, the intrigue of the WordPress
stage lies in the stage itself — as well as in its
enthusiastic network of clients. WordPress-related
Web locales spread a variety of various subjects
identified with the stage, including everything from
instructional exercises to news, and even a little tattle,
if that is your flavor.
Try not to give the volume of clients a chance to trick
you: WordPress has gloating rights to the most
supportive blogging network on the Web. Try not to
stress in case you're not an individual from the
WordPress people group. Joining is simple: Simply
start your very own blog by utilizing the WordPress
stage. In case you're as of now blogging on an

alternate stage, for example, Blogspot or Movable Type, WordPress makes moving your information from that stage to another WordPress arrangement straightforward. The help gatherings are facilitated on the WordPress.org Web webpage, yet don't hope to locate any official type of help from the WordPress engineers. Rather, you locate a huge network of individuals from varying backgrounds looking for answers and giving arrangements. Clients from novice and fledgling level to the most developed level peruse the discussions offering help for each other. Every client has their very own encounters, issues, and information level with WordPress, and the help gatherings are the place they share those encounters and search out the encounters of different clients. Remember that the individuals you find and connect with on these official gatherings are offering their insight on a volunteer premise just — thus, as usual, basic politeness principles apply. Utilizing "please" and "thank you" go a long, long path in the discussions. In the event that you discover arrangements and help with the WordPress bolster gatherings, consider perusing through the discussion passages to see whether you can help another person by responding to an inquiry or two. The WordPress Codex is a community exertion to report the utilization of the WordPress software. All supporters of the Codex are WordPress clients who give their time as a method for offering back to the free, open source venture that has given them a powerful bit of software for distributing unreservedly on the Web. You have enormous designs for your blog, and your time is profitable. Enlisting an expert to deal with the back-end plan and upkeep of your blog empowers you to invest your energy making the content and building your readership on the front end.

Numerous bloggers who choose to go the custom course by enlisting a structure proficient do it for another explanation: They need the plans/subjects of their online journals to be extraordinary. Free subjects are pleasant, yet you run the hazard that your blog will look like several different web journals out there. A brand, a term frequently utilized in publicizing and showcasing, alludes to the unmistakable personality of an item — for this situation, your blog. Having a one of a kind brand or structure for your site sets yours separated from the rest. On the off chance that your blog has a custom look, individuals will connect that look with you. You can achieve marking with a solitary logo or a whole format and shading plan based on your personal preference.

WordPress designers can take a straightforward blog and transform it into something dynamic, delightful, and energizing. These individuals are specialists in the visual communication, CSS styling, and layout labeling expected to make an interesting topic for your Web webpage. Frequently, WordPress designers are talented in introducing and redesigning WordPress software and modules; some of the time, they're even gifted in making custom PHP or modules. These people are the ones you need to contact when you're searching for somebody to make a pleasant, special plan for your Web webpage that is an individual, visual expansion of you or your organization.

Some blog designers post their rates on their Web locales since they offer plan bundles, while different designer's statement extends on a case-by-case premise in light of the fact that each task is extraordinary. When you're looking for a planner, if the costs aren't shown on the site, simply drop the originator an email and request a gauge. Equipped with this data, you can do a little correlation shopping while you scan for simply the correct originator. Nobody knows this superior to the amazingly capable blog engineers in the center WordPress improvement group. An engineer can take a portion of the basic code, make somewhat enchantment occur among PHP and the MySQL database that stores the content of your blog, and make a unique showcase of that content for you. In all probability, you'll contact a designer when you need to accomplish something with your blog that is somewhat strange and you can't discover a module that works.

In the event that you've experienced all the accessible WordPress modules and still can't locate the accurate capacity that you need your WordPress blog to perform, get in touch with one of these people. Clarify what you need. The engineer can disclose to you whether it very well may be done, regardless of whether she is accessible to do it, and the amount it will cost (remember that part!).

Blog consultants will be unable to structure or code for you, yet they're presumably associated with individuals who can. Consultants can enable you to accomplish your objectives for your blog as far as online perceivability, promoting plans, and site improvement. A large portion of these people can enable you to discover how to profit with your blog and interface you with different publicizing programs. Honestly, you can do what blog consultants do by contributing only a brief period and research in these regions. Similarly as with structure and coding, nonetheless, making sense of everything and after that actualizing it requires some investment. In some cases, it's simpler — and more practical — to enlist an expert instead of do it without anyone else's help.

1.9 Different Versions of WordPress

Bloggers have an abundance of software stages to look over. You need to be certain that the stage you pick has every one of the choices you're searching for. WordPress is special in that it offers two versions of its software. Every form is intended to meet the different needs of bloggers.

WordPress.com is a facilitated arrangement, which means it has no software necessity, no downloads, and no establishment or server designs. Everything's accomplished for you toward the back, in the background. You don't need to stress over how the procedure occurs; it happens rapidly, and before you know it, you're making your first blog entry by utilizing a WordPress.com blog arrangement.

WordPress.com has a few constraints, be that as it may. It won't let you introduce modules or custom topics, for instance, or redo the base code documents. WordPress.com offers some customization with its custom CSS highlight — however that is certainly not a free administration; you need to pay for the overhaul. WordPress.com offers a few overhauls to help make your blogging life simpler.

Indeed, even with its restrictions, WordPress.com is a magnificent beginning stage and prologue to the universe of WordPress, in case you're new to blogging and somewhat threatened by the design prerequisites of oneself introduced WordPress.org software.

Fortunately in the event that you exceed your WordPress.com-facilitated blog and need to move to oneself facilitated WordPress.org software, you can. You can even take all the content from your WordPress.com-facilitated blog with you and effectively import it into your new arrangement with the WordPress.org software. Hence, when it's all said and done, your choices aren't generally that restricted. WordPress.org is simply the introduced, self-facilitated software adaptation of WordPress you introduce on a Web server that you have set up on an area you have enlisted. Except if you possess your very own Web server, you have to rent one. Renting space on a Web server is Web facilitating, and except if you know somebody who knows somebody, facilitating by and large isn't free.

CHAPTER 2: SETTING WORDPRESS SOFTWARE

2.1 System Requirements Understanding

Before you can begin blogging with WordPress, you need to set up your base camp. Doing so includes more than essentially downloading and introducing the WordPress software. You additionally need to build up your space (your blog address) and your Web facilitating administration (the spot that houses your blog). In spite of the fact that you at first download your WordPress software onto your hard drive, you introduce it on a Web have.

On the off chance that you have never used WordPress, you should initially think about numerous components, just as adapt to an expectation to absorb information, since setting up your blog through a facilitating administration includes utilizing a few advancements that you may not feel good with. This part takes you through the nuts and bolts of those innovations, and by the last page of this section, you'll have WordPress effectively introduced on a Web server with your own space name.

The initial moves toward introducing and setting up a WordPress blog are settling on a choice about a space name and afterward buying the enrollment of that name through an area recorder. An area name is the novel Web address that you type in a Web program's location bar to visit a Web webpage.

When enrolling a space name, know about the expansion that you need. The .com, .net, .organization, .data, or .business augmentation that you see labeled on to the part of the arrangement name is the top-level area expansion. When you register your area name, you're approached to pick the augmentation you need for your space (as long as it's accessible, that is).

A useful piece of advise here: Just in light of the fact that you enrolled your space as a .com doesn't imply that another person doesn't, or can't, claim the exceptionally same area name with a .net. So, on the off chance that you register MyDogHasFleas.com, and the website turns out to be massively well known among readers with canines that have insects, another person can tag along, register MyDogHasFleas.net, and run a comparable webpage to yours in the expectation of riding the coattails of your Web website's ubiquity and readership. In the event that you need to deflect this issue, you can enlist your space name with every single accessible expansion.

Enrolling a space costs you somewhere in the range of $3 to $30 every year, contingent upon what administration you use for an enlistment center and what alternatives, (for example, security choices and web crawler accommodation administrations) you apply to your area name during the enlistment procedure.

When you pay the space enrollment charge today, you have to pay another enlistment expense when the reestablishment date comes up again in a year, or two, or five — anyway numerous years you enrolled your area name for. Most enlistment centers give you the alternative of pursuing an administration called Auto Renew to naturally restore your space name and bill the charges to the Visa you set up on that account. The enlistment center sends you an update a couple of months ahead of time, disclosing to you it's a great opportunity to reestablish. On the off chance that you don't have Auto Renew set up, you have to sign in to your enlistment center record before it terminates and physically restore your space name.

Area recorders are affirmed and endorsed by the Internet Corporation for Appointed Names and Numbers (ICANN). Albeit several area recorders exist, the ones in the accompanying rundown are well known on account of their life span in the business, aggressive estimating, and the assortment of administrations they offer notwithstanding space name enlistment. After you register your area, you have to discover a spot for it to live — a Web have. Web facilitating is the second bit of the riddle that you have to finish before you start working with WordPress.org.

A Web host is a business, a gathering, or a person that gives Web server space and data transmission for document move to Web website proprietors who don't have it. For the most part, Web facilitating administrations charge a month to month or yearly expense — except if you're lucky enough to realize somebody who will give you server space and transfer speed free. The expense shifts from host to have, however you can get quality Web facilitating administrations for $3 to $10 every month to begin. When examining Web facilitating contemplations, it is essential to comprehend where your facilitating record closures and WordPress starts. Backing for the WordPress software could conceivably be incorporated into your facilitating bundle.

Some Web hosts consider WordPress to be an outsider application. This implies the host normally won't give specialized help on the utilization of WordPress (or some other software application) since software support by and large is excluded in your facilitating bundle. The Web host underpins your facilitating account in any case, regularly, doesn't bolster the software you introduce. Then again, if your Web host underpins the software for you, it includes some major disadvantages: You need to pay for that additional help. To discover whether your picked host bolsters WordPress, ask first.

A couple of Web facilitating suppliers offer free space name enlistment when you pursue facilitating administrations. Research this theme and read their terms of administration since that free space name may accompany conditions. Huge numbers of our customers have gone this course, just to discover a couple of months after the fact that the Web facilitating supplier has full control of the area name, and the customer can't move that space off the host's servers, either for a set period (generally, a year or two) or for interminability. It's in every case best to have the control in your grasp, not somebody else's, so attempt to stay with a free space recorder, for example, Network Solutions.

Most Web facilitating suppliers give you access to a facilitating account chief that enables you to sign in to your Web facilitating record to oversee administrations. cPanel is maybe the most prominent management interface, yet Plesk and NetAdmin are still broadly utilized. These administration interfaces provide you access to server logs where you can view such things as bandwidth and hard plate use. Start checking those things once in a while to ensure that you stay educated about how much use your site is utilizing.

Beginning with a self-facilitated WordPress blog doesn't take much circle space by any means. A decent beginning stage for circle space is between 3–5GB of extra room. On the off chance that you find that you need extra space, contact your facilitating supplier for an update in space.

Bandwidth alludes to the measure of information that is conveyed from indicate A point B inside a particular period (generally, one moment or two). I live out in the nation — essentially the center of no place. The water that goes to my home is given by a private well that untruths covered in the terrace some place. Between my home and the well are channels that carry the water to my home. The channels give a free progression of water to our home with the goal that everybody can make the most of their long, hot showers while I work over dishes and clothing, all simultaneously.

Web hosts are quite liberal with the measure of bandwidth they give in their bundles. Like plate space, bandwidth is estimated in gigabytes (GB). Bandwidth arrangement of 10–50GB is commonly a decent add up to run a Web website with a blog.

2.2 File Transfer Protocol

All through this whole book, you keep running into the term FTP. What's FTP? FTP is a network protocol used to duplicate files starting with one host then onto the next over the Internet. With FTP, you can perform different errands, including transferring and downloading WordPress files, altering files, and changing authorizations on files.

FTP projects are alluded to as FTP customers or FTP customer software. Whatever you choose to call it, a FTP customer is software that you use to interface with your Web server to see, open, alter, and transfer files to and from your Web server. On the off chance that you utilize an alternate FTP customer software than FileZilla, the means and look of the software will contrast, and you should adjust your means and practice for the particular FTP customer software you are utilizing.

Since your neighborhood PC is associated with your Web server, transferring files between the two couldn't be simpler. Inside the FTP customer software, you can peruse the registries and envelopes on your neighborhood PC on the left side and peruse the indexes and organizers on your Web server on the correct side.

FTP customers make it simple to transfer files from your PC to your facilitating account by utilizing an intuitive technique. Two strategies for transferring files are:

By and large, transferring files from your neighborhood PC to your Web server. To transfer a file from your PC to your Web server, click the file you need to transfer from your neighborhood PC and simplified it onto the correct side (the Web server side).

Conveying files from your Web server to your nearby PC. To transfer a file from your Web server to your nearby PC, click the file you need to transfer from your Web server and intuitive it onto to one side (the neighborhood PC side).

When you alter files by utilizing the FTP alter highlight, you are altering files in a "live" domain; implying that when you spare the progressions and transfer the file, the progressions produce results quickly and influence your live Web webpage. Hence, we firmly suggest downloading a duplicate of the first file to your neighborhood PC before making changes. That way, on the off chance that you happen to make a grammatical mistake on the spared file and your Web website goes haywire, you have a duplicate of the first to transfer to reestablish it to its unique state.

Regularly, envelopes and files inside your Web server are appointed consents of either 644 or 755. As a rule, you'll see PHP files, or files that end with the .php augmentation, with authorizations set to 644 if the Web server is arranged to utilize PHP Safe Mode.

You may keep running over a circumstance where you're approached to alter and change the file consents on a specific file on your Web server. With WordPress destinations, this typically happens when managing modules or subject files that require files or envelopes to be writable by the Web server. This training is alluded to as CHMOD, an abbreviation for Change Mode. When somebody says, "You have to CHMOD that file to 755," you'll recognize what they are discussing.

2.3 What are PHP and MySQL?

WordPress utilizes a PHP/MySQL stage, which gives all that you have to make your very own blog and distribute your own content progressively, without realizing how to program those pages. To put it plainly, all your content is put away in a MySQL database in your facilitating account.

PHP is a server-side scripting language for making dynamic Web pages. At the point when a guest opens a page worked in PHP, the server forms the PHP directions and after that sends the outcomes to the guest's program. MySQL is an open source social database management system (RDBMS) that utilizations Structured Query Language (SQL), the most prevalent language for including, getting to, and handling information in a database. In the event that that all seems like Greek to you, simply consider MySQL a major file bureau where all the content on your blog is put away.

Each time a guest goes to your blog to peruse your content, he makes a solicitation that is sent to a host server. The PHP programming language gets that demand, makes a call to the MySQL database, gets the mentioned data from the database, and afterward exhibits the mentioned data to your guest through his Web program.

Here content alludes to the information put away in the MySQL database; that is, your blog entries, pages, remarks, connections, and alternatives that you set up in the WordPress Dashboard. Be that as it may, the subject (or structure) you use for your blog — regardless of whether it's the default topic, one you make, or one you have hand crafted — isn't a piece of the content for this situation. Topic files are a piece of the file system and aren't put away in the database. In this way, it's a smart thought to make and keep a reinforcement of any topic files that you're at present utilizing.

WordPress requires PHP so as to work; in this way, your Web facilitating supplier must have PHP empowered on your Web server. In the event that you as of now have WordPress ready for action on your Web webpage, you know PHP is running and working fine and dandy. As of now, the PHP rendition required for WordPress is adaptation 4.3 or later. As we state prior, WordPress is situated in PHP (a scripting language for making Web pages) and uses PHP directions to pull data from the MySQL database. Each label starts with the capacity to begin PHP and finishes with a capacity to stop it. In those two directions experience the solicitation to the database that advises WordPress to snatch the information and show it.

Each PHP direction you start requires a stop order. For each <?php, you should incorporate the end ?> order some place later in the code. PHP directions organized inappropriately cause monstrous blunders on your site, and they've been known to send software engineers, designers, and facilitating suppliers into noisy shouting fits. You discover a great deal of beginning and halting of PHP all through the WordPress formats and capacities. The procedure appears just as it would be resource concentrated, if not comprehensive, yet it truly isn't.

Numerous new WordPress clients are threatened by the MySQL database, maybe on the grounds that it is by all accounts route over their specialized aptitudes or capacities. Believe it or not, ordinary clients of WordPress — the individuals who simply use it to distribute content — don't generally ever need to dive into the database except if they need to. You possibly need to investigate the database in case you're managing subject or module advancement, or with contributing code to the WordPress venture.

2.4 WordPress Installation

Fantastico is a well known script installer that few Web facilitating suppliers make accessible to their customers. Fantastico contains various sorts of scripts and projects that you can introduce on your facilitating account, strikingly, the WordPress programming. Fantastico is an outsider script that exists as an extra to cPanel.

Web hosts buy in to Fantastico and add it to your cPanel as an additional administration for you to exploit; nonetheless, Web facilitating suppliers don't control which scripts, or which forms of scripts, are accessible inside Fantastico. Web hosts are totally reliant upon the producers of Fantastico with respect to what scripts and script variants are accessible. Fantastico is ordinarily about a month or so behind the game when refreshing the projects in its script installer.

On the off chance that you introduce WordPress physically, here's where things become real — that is, you're putting WordPress' well known five-minute installation to the test. Just set your watch and see whether you can comply with that time constraint.

The renowned five-minute installation incorporates just the time it takes to introduce the product. This does exclude an opportunity to enlist an area name;

an opportunity to get and set up your Web facilitating administration; or an opportunity to download, introduce, arrange, and make sense of how to utilize the FTP programming.

The WordPress programming is an individual distributing framework that uses a PHP/MySQL stage, which gives all that you have to make your own blog and distribute your very own substance progressively without realizing how to program those pages. So, all your substance (choices, posts, remarks, and other relevant information) is put away in a MySQL database in your facilitating account.

Each time guests go to your blog to peruse your substance, they make a solicitation that is sent to your server. The PHP programming language gets that demand, gets the mentioned data from the MySQL database, and afterward displays the mentioned data to your guests through their Web programs.

Each Web host is distinctive by the way it gives you access to set up and deal with your MySQL database(s) for your record. On the off chance that your host gives an alternate interface, similar fundamental advances apply; in any case, the arrangement in the interface that your Web host gives might be unique.

An affirmation message shows up expressing that the username was made with the secret word you indicated. For security reasons, ensure that your secret word isn't something that subtle programmers can without much of a stretch estimate. Give your database a name that you'll recollect later. This training is particularly useful in the event that you run more than one MySQL database in your record. For example, in the event that you name a database WordPress or wpblog, you can be sensibly sure in about a year when you need to get to your database to make some arrangement changes that you know precisely which qualifications to utilize.

Ensure that you note the database name, username, and secret word that you set up during this procedure. You need them in the area "Running the installation script" later in this section before formally introducing WordPress on your Web server. Note them on a bit of paper, or reorder them into a content manager window; in any case, ensure that you have them helpful.

The MySQL database for your WordPress Web webpage is finished and you're prepared to continue to the last advance of introducing the product on your Web server. WordPress gives both of you pressure positions for the product: .zip and .tar.gz. We suggest getting the Zip record since it's the most widely recognized configuration for compacted documents and the two Windows and Mac operating systems can utilize the arrangement. By and large, the .tar.gz document arrangement is utilized for Unix operating systems.

Download the WordPress programming to your PC and afterward decompress (unload or unfasten) it to an envelope on your PC's hard drive. These means start the installation procedure for WordPress. Having the program without anyone else PC isn't sufficient, nonetheless. You additionally need to transfer (or transfer) it to your Web server account.

Before you introduce WordPress on your Web server, you have to ensure that you have the MySQL database set up and prepared to acknowledge the WordPress installation. Be certain that you've pursued the former strides to set up your MySQL database before continuing.

Generally, it's a sure thing to ensure that the transfer method of your FTP customer is set to autodetect. Be that as it may, in the event that you experience issues with how those records load on your site, retransfer the documents by utilizing the suitable transfer mode. The WordPress installation machine does something amazing and makes every one of the tables inside the database that contain the default information for your blog. WordPress shows the login data you have to get to the WordPress Dashboard. Make note of this username and secret word before you leave this page. Scrawl them on a bit of paper or duplicate them into a content tool, for example, Notepad.

Then, proceed and click the Install WordPress button. Now you're sent an email with the login data and login URL. This data is convenient in case you're summoned during this piece of the installation procedure. So feel free to allow them to ask out, pick up the telephone, blend some espresso, or take a 15-

minute power snooze. In the event that you by one way or another make tracks in an opposite direction from this page, the email sent to you contains the data you have to sign in to your WordPress blog.

2.5 Optimum Performance and Security Configurations

As you can most likely as of now surmise, programmers locate the profitable data put away in the wp-config.php record alluring. In the event that somebody with odious purpose were to get your database username and secret phrase, he could sign in and fix everything that you've constructed! Accordingly, make whatever strides you can to verify that record with the goal that nobody, yet you, approaches it. One snappy and simple approach to do that is to deny any bots (robotized programming applications that keep running on the Internet) access to it and to change the record authorizations.

After the wp-config.php record is pleasant and secure, you have to realize what's put away inside it so you can reference it and see how WordPress guides into, or speaks with, the database you arranged and set up. Open the wp-config.php record by utilizing your default word processor and view. The following segments take you through, in detail, the data put away inside.

The database data area of the wp-config.php document contains the database certifications that are required for WordPress to associate with your database. During installation, the WordPress installation script populates this information after you input the database name, username, secret key, and host in the installation structure.

Secret keys improve WordPress security through client validation with the situation of a treat in the client's Web program. They are additionally alluded to as salts, a word ordinarily utilized in cryptography to speak to irregular keys, for example, in a secret phrase. Secret keys in your wp-config.php record make your site harder for outside sources to access since they add arbitrary keys to the client secret word. These values aren't generated during the WordPress installation, so after the installation is finished, you have to visit the wp-config.php document to set the keys with the goal that your WordPress installation has novel keys that are not the same as some other installation — making it secure over time, in light of the fact that the keys are explicit just to your site.

You can change the secret keys whenever by altering the wp-config.php record and supplanting the keys with new ones. Doing so doesn't influence the working of your Web webpage, yet it requires that clients sign in to your website once more, in the event that they were at that point signed in, on the grounds that changing the keys changes client verification and resigns the treats that had just been set in their programs.

During the installation procedure, you can change the default wp_ prefix to anything you need. Actually, most security specialists suggest that you change the database prefix in light of the fact that WordPress is a major objective for hacking (malevolent scripts, spam, etc). Web bots and arachnids can be set to search for the standard WordPress default settings and endeavor to misuse them. The wp_ table prefix is one of those conspicuous default settings, so to shield your installation, change the prefix to anything you pick. Anyway, remember that in the event that you change the prefix, you have to transform it to something hard for a script or a computerized program to figure.

You can move the/wp-content registry to an area on your Web server outside the WordPress installation catalog, making it significantly harder, if certainly feasible, for outside programmers to find. To move the envelope, make another organizer on your Web server outside the WordPress installation index and afterward, utilizing your FTP program, simplified the/wp-content organizer to the enhanced one you just made. In most well known FTP programs, you can right-click with your mouse and pick New Folder, which enables you to make another envelope and give it a name.

WordPress autosaves updates of your posts and pages, and you can send presents and pages on the waste can, rather than totally erasing them. You visit the garbage can and for all time erase your posts or pages. This additional progression is a protect in the event of slip-ups.

WordPress makes these modifications through the Autosave include. As a matter of course, WordPress consequently spares a post amendment consistently. In the event that you set aside a long effort to compose a post, you could pile on many post modifications, which are put away in the database and occupy space.

Some facilitating suppliers debilitate the capacity to expand PHP memory restrains on your Web facilitating account, so relying upon your facilitating condition, your endeavors to build as far as possible may not work. On the off chance that you find this is the situation for your specific facilitating account, you can contact your host and request that he increment the PHP memory limit for your record or change to an alternate facilitating supplier.

A decent method to improve the speed of your Web website is through caching various kinds of substance. Caching substance intends to store it straightforwardly with the goal that it very well may be utilized for future heaps of your Web website. A decent caching framework for your Web website gathers all the Web pages on your webpage and duplicates, stores, and conveys the documents to guests of your Web webpage. This essentially diminishes the server load in light of the fact that without it, WordPress makes pages on your Web website progressively — each time a guest stacks your Web webpage, calls are made to the database and code is gone along and executed each opportunity to make the page in her program. On the off chance that you utilize a decent caching system, those documents are as of now assembled and showed, so your Web server doesn't have to revamp those pages each time.

2.6 WordPress Upgrading

Before upgrading your WordPress programming installation, ensure you back up your database. This progression isn't required, obviously, however it's a savvy venture to take to defend your Web website and guarantee you have a total duplicate of your Web webpage information if your redesign turns out badly.

cPanel is a Web hosting interface given by many Web has as a Web hosting account the executives device that contains phpMyAdmin as the favored device to use to oversee and direct databases. Not all Web hosts use cPanel or phpMyAdmin, nonetheless, so if yours doesn't, you have to counsel the client documentation for the devices that your Web host gives.

The second and least utilized strategy for upgrading WordPress is the manual technique. The technique is least utilized chiefly in light of the fact that the programmed strategy, examined in the former area, is so fast and simple to achieve. Be that as it may, certain conditions — presumably identified with the powerlessness of your hosting condition to oblige the programmed strategy — exist where you can physically update WordPress.

The redesign procedure happens all the time, in any event three or four times each year. For certain clients, this is a baffling truth of utilizing WordPress; be that as it may, this dynamic advancement condition is a piece of what makes WordPress the most famous stage accessible. Since WordPress is continually including incredible new highlights and capacities to the stage, upgrading consistently guarantees that you're over the game and utilizing the most recent devices and highlights.

2.7 Backup, Packup and Switching to a New Host

WordPress gives you a chance to move your blog from such stages as Blogspot, TypePad, and Movable Type. It additionally gives you a clever method to move from any blogging stage by means of RSS channels, as long as the stage you're bringing in from has a RSS channel accessible. A few stages, for example, MySpace, have a few constraints on RSS channel accessibility, so make certain to check with your foundation supplier.

For each blogging stage, the WordPress.org stage gives you a fast and simple approach to introduce plugins that enables you to import and utilize your substance immediately. The shippers are bundled in a plugin group in light of the fact that a great many people utilize a merchant just once, and a few people don't utilize the merchant apparatuses by any means. The plugins are there for you to utilize on the off chance that you need them. WordPress.com, then again, has the merchants incorporated with the product. Note the distinctions for the form you are utilizing.

The facilitated adaptation of WordPress.com and oneself facilitated rendition of WordPress.org enable you to relocate your blog to their foundation; be that as it may, WordPress.com doesn't give the same number of alternatives to import as WordPress. organization does.

This import script takes into account a greatest document size of 128MB. In the event that you get an "out of memory" blunder, take a stab at isolating the import record into pieces and transferring them independently. The import script is shrewd enough to overlook copy sections, so on the off chance that you have to run the script a couple of times to get it to take everything, you can do as such without too much stress over copying your substance.

Each blogging project has a remarkable method for conveying substance and information to your blog. Layout labels differ from program to program; no two are the equivalent, and every format document requires transformation in the event that you need to utilize your layout with your new WordPress blog.

To utilize your very own layout, ensure that you spared all the format documents, the pictures, and the template from your past blog arrangement. You need them to change over the template(s) for use in WordPress.

Many free templates are accessible for use with WordPress, so it might be significantly simpler to relinquish the format you're presently working with and locate a free WordPress layout that you like. On the off chance that you paid to have a specially craft accomplished for your blog, contact the creator of your topic, and contract him to play out the layout change for you. On the other hand, you can procure a few WordPress specialists to play out the change for you — including yours really.

Both WordPress.com and WordPress.org offer an import script for LiveJournal clients, and the way toward bringing in from LiveJournal to WordPress is the equivalent for every stage. LiveJournal gives you a chance to trade the XML documents each month in turn, so in the event that you have a blog with a while of posts, be set up to be at this procedure for some time. To start with, you need to send out the sections each month in turn, and after that you need to bring them into WordPress — that's right, you got it — each month in turn.

To speed the procedure a bit, you can spare all the sent out XML LiveJournal records in a single book report by reordering every month's XML document into one plain-content record (made in a word processor, for example, Notepad), in this manner making one long XML record with every one of the posts from your LiveJournal blog. At that point you can spare the record as a XML document to set it up for import into your WordPress blog. Six Apart made both Movable Type and TypePad. This import script moves all your blog entries, remarks, and trackbacks to your WordPress blog.

At the point when the import script completes, you can allot clients to the posts, coordinating the Movable Type or TypePad usernames with WordPress usernames. In the event that you have only one creator on each blog, this procedure is simple; you essentially dole out your WordPress login to the Movable Type or TypePad username by utilizing the drop-down menu. On the off chance that you have various creators on the two web journals, coordinate the Movable Type or TypePad usernames with the right WordPress login names and afterward snap Save Changes.

When in doubt, or if WordPress doesn't give an import script that you requirement for your present blog stage, you can import your blog information by means of the RSS channel for the blog you need to import. With the RSS import technique, you can import posts no one but; you can't utilize this strategy to import remarks, trackbacks, classifications, or clients. WordPress.com as of now doesn't give you a chance to import blog information by means of a RSS channel; this capacity works just with oneself facilitated WordPress.org stage.

There may come a period that you choose you have to change from your current hosting supplier to another one. There are reasons why somebody would need to do this — it is possible that you're discontent with your present supplier and need to move to another one, or your present supplier is leaving business and you're compelled to move. Transferring starting with one host then onto the next is a reality that some Web webpage proprietors must face, and transferring a current Web website, with the majority of its substance, records, and information, starting with one host then onto the next can appear to be an overwhelming errand.

BackupBuddy is a plugin that moves a WordPress Web webpage starting with one hosting condition then onto the next. This plugin isn't free or accessible in the WordPress Plugin Directory, yet it merits each penny since it takes the whole reinforcement and relocation procedure and makes mincemeat out of it — which means, it makes moving the site simple to achieve and should be possible in minutes rather than hours.

CHAPTER 3: WORPRESS DASHBOARD

3.1 Logging in

The cookie advises WordPress to recollect your login qualifications whenever you appear. The cookie set by WordPress is innocuous and stores your WordPress login on your PC. As a result of the cookie, WordPress recollects that you whenever you visit. Furthermore, on the grounds that this alternative advises the program to recall your login, we don't exhort checking this choice on open PCs. Abstain from choosing Remember Me when you're utilizing your work PC or a PC at an Internet bistro.

You can change how the WordPress Dashboard looks, at any rate regarding the request the modules show up on it. You can extend (open) and breakdown (close) the individual modules by clicking your mouse anyplace inside the dark title bar of the module. This component is extremely decent in light of the fact that you can utilize the Dashboard for simply those modules that you use normally. The idea is simple: Keep the modules you utilize all the time open and close the ones that you utilize just at times — you can open those modules just when you truly need them. You spare space and can modify your Dashboard to suit your needs.

The navigation menu in the WordPress Dashboard shows up on the left half of your program window. When you have to return to the WordPress Dashboard, click the Dashboard connect that shows up at the highest point of the navigation menu of any of the pages inside your WordPress Dashboard.

Approaching links records all the blog-clever individuals who composed a blog entry that links to your blog. At the point when your blog is shiny new, you won't perceive any approaching links recorded in this area. Try not to surrender, in any case; over the long haul, you'll see this posting of links top off while an ever increasing number of individuals find you and your motivated compositions! The Plugins module incorporates three titles of WordPress plugins that are connected to its individual module page inside the WordPress Plugin Directory. The Plugins module pulls data by means of RSS channel from the authority WordPress Plugin Directory.

In case you're utilizing a fresh out of the plastic new WordPress blog and this is another establishment, the Recent Drafts module shows the message There Are No Drafts at the Moment since you haven't composed any drafts. Over the long haul, be that as it may, and you compose a couple of posts in your blog, you may spare a portion of those presents as drafts — on be altered and distributed later. Those drafts appear in the Recent Drafts module.

WordPress is about client experience, be that as it may, so you can change the alternatives to indicate what shows up around there. You can change the things in this module similarly that you change the choices for the WordPress Development Blog module

3.2 Dashboard Customization

You can organize the request for the modules in your Dashboard to suit your preferences. WordPress puts a lot of accentuation on client experience, and a major piece of that exertion brings about your capacity to make a Dashboard that you find generally helpful. You can undoubtedly change the modules to show and the request in which they show.

Rehash these means with every module that you need to proceed onward the Dashboard by relocating them so they show up in the request you like. When you explore away from the Dashboard, WordPress recollects the progressions you made. When you return, despite everything you see your tweaked Dashboard, and you don't have to re-try these adjustments later on.

We're sure that everybody works in an unexpected way, as far as how we like our workspace spread out. By and by, Lisa likes to have one long section of things so she can look through and center around one territory, specifically, without different things to one side and left of her borders.

By utilizing the highlights that empower you to alter your Dashboard, you can make your own, individualized workspace that works best for you, in light of how you use WordPress. With these highlights, everybody can modify his own WordPress experience, and no two WordPress client encounters are essentially the equivalent — like snowflakes!

The engineers of the WordPress programming truly invest energy and exertion to give clients huge amounts of inline documentation that gives a few hints and indications directly inside the Dashboard. You can for the most part find inline documentation for almost every WordPress highlight you'll utilize.

Inline documentation alludes to those little sentences or expressions that you see close by or underneath an element in WordPress that give a short, however exceptionally accommodating, and clarification about what the element is. Notwithstanding the inline documentation that you find dispersed all through the Dashboard, an accommodating Help tab is situated in the upper-right corner of your Dashboard. The inline documentation, and the points and content you find in the Help tab, exist to help clients while they work with the WordPress stage, helping make the experience as straightforward as could be expected under the circumstances.

All through the various pages of your WordPress Dashboard, you can apply the customization includes that we spread for the principle Dashboard page. Each segment of the WordPress Dashboard is adjustable, with intuitive modules, screen alternatives, and inline help and documentation

3.3 Tools and Settings

After you introduce the WordPress programming and sign in, you can put an individual stamp on your blog by giving it a title and portrayal, setting your contact email address, and distinguishing yourself as the creator of the blog. You deal with these and different settings on the General Settings page.

Snap the Save Changes catch at the base of any page where you set new choices. On the off chance that you don't snap Save Changes, your settings aren't spared, and WordPress returns to the former alternatives. Each time you click the Save Changes catch, WordPress reloads the present page, showing the new alternatives that you simply set.

Dialog is the fourth thing in the Settings menu list; click it to open the Discussion Settings page. The segments on this tab let you set alternatives for dealing with remarks and distributing presents on your blog.

In the Comment Moderation segment, you can set choices to determine what sorts of remarks are held in the balance line to anticipate your endorsement. To keep spammers from spamming your blog with a huge amount of links, enter a number in the Hold a Comment in the Queue If It Contains X or More Links content box. The default number of links permitted is two. Attempt that setting, and on the off chance that you find that you're getting a great deal of spam remarks that contain links, consider dropping that number down to 1, or even 0, to keep those remarks from being distributed on your blog. At times, genuine analysts will incorporate a connection or two in the body of their remark; after an analyst is set apart as endorsed, she is never again influenced by this technique for spam security.

The enormous content box in the Comment Moderation segment gives you a chance to type catchphrases, URLs, email locations, and IP addresses so that on the off chance that they show up in remarks, you need to hold those remarks in the control line for your endorsement.

By and large, you need web indexes to have the option to discover your blog. Nonetheless, on the off chance that you have exceptional conditions, you might need to authorize your security settings. For instance, we blocked web indexes for the website we're utilizing to make the figures in this book since we don't need web crawlers to discover it. At the highest point of the site, to one side of the site title, a note says Search Engines Blocked. This note exists just when you have your protection settings set to square web indexes. When you have security empowered, web crawlers and other substance bots can't discover your Web webpage.

Permalinks are intended to be perpetual links to your blog entries (which is the place the perma part of that word originates from, on the off chance that you're pondering). Different bloggers can utilize a post permalink to allude to that specific blog entry. Preferably, the permalink of a post never shows signs of change. WordPress makes the permalink naturally when you distribute another post.

Legitimately beneath the two New Password content boxes is a little secret key partner. WordPress encourages you make a safe secret word. It alarms you if the secret key you picked is excessively short or not verify enough by disclosing to you that it's Bad. When making another secret key, utilize a mix of letters, numbers, and images to make it difficult for anybody to figure.

Change your secret word as often as possible. We can't prescribe this training unequivocally enough. A few people on the Internet make it their business to endeavor to seize sites for their very own vindictive purposes. In the event that you change your secret phrase month to month, you bring down your hazard by keeping programmers speculating.

Notwithstanding setting your own settings in the Dashboard, you can deal with the everyday support of your blog. The accompanying areas take you through the links to these pages in the Dashboard navigation menus.

Remarks in the navigation menu don't have a drop-down rundown of links. You basically snap Comments to open the Comments page, where WordPress gives you the alternatives to see.

3.4 User Management

Multi-author blogging means welcoming others to coauthor, or contribute articles, posts, pages, or other substance to your blog. You can extend the contributions on your Web webpage or blog by utilizing multi-author blogging on the grounds that you can have a few unique individuals composing on various points or offering alternate points of view on a similar theme. Numerous individuals use it to make a synergistic composition space on the Web, and WordPress doesn't confine you in the quantity of authors you can add to your blog.

Moreover, bloggers can welcome other individuals to enroll as endorsers, who don't contribute content however are enlisted individuals from the blog, which can have benefits, as well.

At the point when clients register on your Web website, you, as the Administrator, get an email notice, so you generally know when new clients register, and you would then be able to go into your Dashboard and alter the client to set his job any way you see fit. WordPress requests that you type the password twice as a method for verifying the password (ensuring that you composed it accurately the first run through). WordPress gives a quality marker that gives you a thought of how solid, or secure, your picked password is. You need secure passwords with the goal that nobody can without much of a stretch conjecture them, so make the password in any event seven characters in length and utilize a blend of letters, numbers, and symbols.

After clients register and subside into their records on your site, you, as the site Administrator, can alter their records. You may never need to alter client accounts; be that as it may, you have the choice on the off chance that you need it. Frequently, clients can get to the subtleties of their own records and change email addresses, names, passwords, etc; be that as it may, conditions under which a site head may need to alter client records is get things done.

You may love running a multi-author site, yet it has its difficulties. The moment you become the proprietor of a multi-author site, you quickly expect the job of chief for the authors you welcomed into your space. Now and again, those authors seek you for help and direction, on their substance the board, yet additionally for tips and guidance about how to utilize the WordPress interface — it really is great that you have this book good to go so you can present the pearls of data you're finding inside these pages!

One approach to work an effective multi-author blog includes accepting each open door to advance your authors and their data however much as could reasonably be expected. Authors frequently engage in posting content on other Web destinations, notwithstanding yours, for presentation, and the plugins in this rundown give you instruments to advance authors profiles, links, informal organization nourishes

3.5 Handling Comments

One of the most energizing parts of blogging with WordPress is getting criticism from your readers the minute you make a post to your blog. Criticism, otherwise called blog remarks, is much the same as having a guestbook on your blog.

Individuals leave notes for you that are distributed to your site, and through these notes, you can react and draw in your readers in discussion about the subject. Having this capacity in your blog enables you to grow the musings and thoughts you present in your blog posts by allowing readers the chance to include their input's.

Some blog clients state that a blog without remarks isn't a blog at all on the grounds that the purpose of having a blog, in certain personalities, is to encourage correspondence and connection between the webpage authors and the readers. This conviction is normal in the blogging network in light of the fact that encountering guest criticism by means of remarks is a piece of what's made blogging so mainstream. Be that as it may, permitting remarks is an individual decision, and you don't need to do it on the off chance that you would prefer not to.

Permitting remarks on your blog lets group of spectators individuals effectively include themselves in your blog by making a discourse and exchange about your substance. For the most part, readers find remarking a fantastic encounter when they visit blogs since remarks make them part of the exchange.

On the off chance that you need to fabricate a network of individuals who return to your webpage as often as possible, react to however many remarks that your readers leave on your blog as would be prudent. At the point when individuals set aside the effort to leave you a remark on your substance, they like to realize that you're understanding it and they value hearing your criticism to them. In addition, it keeps discourses vivacious and dynamic on your site.

In specific situations, you might not have any desire to enable readers to leave remarks uninhibitedly on your site. For instance, on the off chance that you composed a blog post on a theme that is viewed as extremely dubious, you might not have any desire to welcome remarks in light of the fact that the subject may prompt fire wars, or remarks that are offending to you, or your readers. In case you're not inspired by the perspective or criticism of readers on your site, or if your substance doesn't generally fit peruser input, you may choose to deny remarks totally.

In the WordPress Dashboard, you have full managerial authority over who can and can't leave remarks. Moreover, on the off chance that somebody leaves a remark that has flawed substance, you can alter the remark or erase it. You're likewise allowed to prohibit remarks on your blog. The Discussion Settings page in your Dashboard contains every one of the settings for permitting, or denying, remarks on your site.

The most ideal approach to comprehend trackbacks is to consider them remarks, aside from a certain something: Trackbacks are remarks left on your blog by different blogs, not by real individuals. In spite of the fact that this procedure may sound baffling, it's quite sensible.

A trackback happens when you make a post on your blog and, inside that post, you give connect to a post made by another blogger in an alternate blog. When you distribute that post, your blog sends a kind of electronic reminder to the blog you connected to. That blog gets the reminder and posts an affirmation of receipt in a remark inside the post that you connected to on their webpage.

That update is sent by means of a system ping (an apparatus used to test, or check, regardless of whether a connection is reachable over the Internet) from your webpage to the website you connect to. This procedure fills in as long as the two blogs support trackback convention. Trackbacks can likewise go to your website by method for a pingback — which, truly, is a similar thing as a trackback, however the wording differs from blog stage to blog stage.

On the off chance that you have your alternatives set with the goal that remarks aren't distributed to your blog until you affirm them, you can support remarks from the Comments page, also. Simply click the Pending connects to list the remarks that are pending control. On the off chance that you have remarks as well as trackbacks anticipating balance, they show up on this page, and you can favor them, mark them as spam, or erase them.

WordPress promptly advises you of any remarks sitting in the control line, anticipating your activity. This notice, which shows up on each and every page, is a little circle, or air pocket, in the left navigation menu, to one side of Comments.

3.6 Link Lists Development

Having an enormous rundown of links underneath the Blogroll heading is simply excessively nonexclusive, and you might need to show gatherings of links with various headings that further characterize them. Like with posts, you can make multiple classes for your links in the WordPress Dashboard on the off chance that you need to have more than one connection list. Giving a depiction further characterizes the class for your readers. You can make the depiction as short or as long as you need. Some WordPress subjects are set up to really show the class portrayal straightforwardly underneath the classification name.

You can alter the links in your blog by tapping the name of the connection you need to alter on the Links page; the Edit Links page opens. When you first see the Links page, a few links are now allotted to your blog. Naturally, WordPress gives seven links in your connection list. These links go to some accommodating Web destinations that contain data and assets for the WordPress programming. You can erase these links, yet we prescribe sparing them for future reference.

With the various alternatives you have accessible with the Link include (classes, pictures, RSS channels, etc), you can show a basic posting of links in your sidebar by utilizing gadgets, or you can make a full page committed to your links in your Dashboard's connection records.

Some site proprietors utilize the Link highlight to make an out and out connection catalog on their locales, which you can without much of a stretch do by utilizing join classifications, pictures, portrayals, etc. Adhering to the guidelines gave in this section, you can make your connection classifications, add your links to the classes, and afterward show them on a page by utilizing distinctive format labels that are accessible in WordPress.

3.7 Categories and Tags Development

WordPress gives you such a significant number of various approaches to compose, order, and file content on your Web webpage or blog. Bundled inside the WordPress programming is the capacity to consequently keep up ordered, arranged files of your distributing history, which furnishes your Web website guests with various approaches to locate your substance. WordPress utilizes PHP and MySQL innovation to sort and arrange all that you distribute in a request that you and your readers can access by date and class. This filing procedure happens naturally with each post you distribute to your blog.

When you make a post on your WordPress blog, you can document that post under a class that you indicate. This element makes for a clever chronicling framework in which you and your readers can discover articles/posts that you've set inside a particular classification. Articles you post are additionally arranged and sorted out by date (day/month/year) with the goal that you can, without much hassle, find articles that you posted at a specific time. In WordPress, a classification is the thing that you decide to be the primary point of a blog post. By utilizing categories, you can record your blog posts into themes by subject. To improve your readers' encounters in exploring through your blog, WordPress sorts out posts by the categories you dole out to them. Guests can tap the categories they're keen on to see the blog posts you've composed on those specific themes.

Subcategories (otherwise called class youngsters) can further refine the principle classification theme by posting explicit points identified with the fundamental (parent) classification. In your Admin Dashboard, on the Manage Categories page, subcategories show up straightforwardly beneath the fundamental classification.

The default class likewise fills in as sort of a safeguard. In the event that you publish a post to your blog and don't dole out that post to a classification, the post is doled out to the default classification naturally, regardless of what you name the class. Today, tomorrow, one month from now, one year from now — while your blog develops in size and age, proceeding to include new categories further characterizes and chronicles the historical backdrop of your blog posts. You aren't constrained in the quantity of categories and subcategories you can make in your blog.

You can erase a class on your blog by floating your mouse pointer on the title of the classification you need to erase, and after that tapping the Delete connect that shows up underneath the classification title. .

Erasing a classification doesn't erase the posts and links in that classification. Rather, posts in the erased class are reassigned to the Uncategorized classification (or whatever you've named the default classification). You utilize the Tags and the Categories pages in your Dashboard to oversee, alter, and make new labels and categories to which you allot your posts when you distribute them.

CHAPTER 4: PUBLISHING WEBSITE USING WORDPRESS

4.1 Writing a Post

Making a blog post is a great deal like composing an email: You give it a title, you compose the message, and you click a catch to send your words into the world. This area covers the means you take to create and publish a blog post on your webpage. By utilizing the various choices that WordPress gives — like talk choices, categories and labels, for instance — you can arrange each post anyway you like.

Of course, the region where you compose your post is in Visual Editing mode, as demonstrated by the Visual tab that shows up over the text. You can mood killer the Visual Text Editor by clicking Your Profile in the Users drop-down rundown. Deselect the Use the Visual Editor When Writing mark box to mood killer this editor in the event that you need to embed the HTML code in your posts yourself.

On the off chance that you need to implant your own HTML code and avoid the Visual Text Editor, click the HTML tab that appears to one side of the Visual tab. In case you're wanting to type HTML code in your post — for a table or video documents, for instance — you need to tap the HTML tab before you can embed that code. In the event that you don't, the Visual Text Editor organizes your code, and it probably looks not at all like you planned it to. WordPress has a clever, worked in autosave include that spares your work while you're composing and altering another post. In the event that your program accidents or you inadvertently close your program window before you physically spare your post, you can get to it again when you get back.

After you compose the post, you can pick a couple of additional alternatives before you publish it for the whole world to see. These settings apply to the post you're presently taking a shot at — not to any future or past posts. You can discover these alternatives beneath and to one side of the Post text box.

When you wrap up the choices for your post, don't explore away from this page; you haven't yet completely spared your alternatives. The accompanying area on publishing your post covers every one of the choices you requirement for sparing your post settings!

WordPress gives you three choices for sparing or publishing your post when you're finished composition it. The Publish module is situated on the correct side of the Add New (or Edit) Post page. Simply click the title of the Publish module to extend the settings you need.

This alternative is also called a clingy post. Ordinarily, posts are shown in sequential request on your blog, showing the latest post on top. On the off chance that you make a post clingy, it stays at the top, regardless of what number of different posts you make after it. When you need to unstick the post, deselect the Stick This Post to the Front Page check box.

In the event that you need to future-publish this post, you can set the time and date for whenever later on. This element has proved to be useful for Lisa ordinarily. For instance, when you have a get-away arranged and you don't need your blog to abandon refreshes while you're gone, you can compose a couple of posts and set the date for a period later on. Those presents are published on her blog while you're some place tropical, plunging with the fishes.

On the off chance that you snap Publish and for reasons unknown don't see the post show up on the first page of your blog, you likely left the Status drop-down rundown set to Unpublished. Your new post shows up in the draft posts, which you can discover by clicking Edit in the Posts drop-down rundown.

4.2 What are Posts and Pages

Pages, in WordPress, are not the same as posts since they don't get filed the manner in which your blog posts/articles do: They aren't ordered or labeled, don't show up in your posting of late blog posts or date files, and aren't syndicated in the RSS channels accessible on your website — in light of the fact that substance inside pages for the most part doesn't change. Pages are viewed as static or remain solitary substance and exist independently from the chronicled post content on your site. With the page include, you can make a boundless measure of static pages separate from your blog posts. Individuals generally utilize this component to make About Me or Contact Me pages, in addition to other things.

Making a first page is a three-advance procedure: Create a static page, assign that static page as the first page of your webpage, and change the page to resemble a Web website, as opposed to a blog. By utilizing this strategy, you can make boundless quantities of static pages to assemble a whole Web webpage. You don't have to have a blog on this website, except if you need one.

Regularly, you don't see a ton of static pages that have the Comments highlight empowered in light of the fact that pages offer static substance that doesn't for the most part fit a lot of discourse. There are exemptions, nonetheless, for example, a Contact page, which may utilize the Comments highlight as a route for readers to connect with the site proprietor through that particular page. Obviously, the decision is yours to make dependent on the particular needs of your Web website.

Some WordPress topics are designed to utilize a picture (photograph) to speak to each post that you have on your blog. The picture can show up on the home/first page, blog page, chronicles, or anyplace inside the substance show on your Web website. In case you're utilizing a topic that has this alternative, you can undoubtedly characterize a post's thumbnail by tapping the Set Featured Image connect underneath the Featured Image module on the Add New Post page. At that point you can relegate a picture that you've transferred to your site as the included picture for a specific post.

4.3 Photos and Galleries Uploading

The interface that WordPress utilizes for document transfers depends on Adobe Flash. Blaze is a particular arrangement of multimedia innovations modified to deal with media documents on the Web. A few programs and working frameworks aren't designed to deal with Flash-based applications. On the off chance that you experience troubles with the Add an Image window, WordPress gives you a simple option: Click the Browser Uploader interface in the Add an Image window to utilize a non–Flashbased uploader to move your records. WordPress naturally makes little and medium-sized adaptations of the images you transfer through the inherent picture uploader. A thumbnail is a littler variant of the first document. You can alter the size of the thumbnail by tapping the Settings connection and after that tapping the Media menu interface. In the Image Sizes segment of the Media Settings page, assign your ideal stature and width of the little and medium thumbnail images created by WordPress. When you transfer your picture, you can set its arrangement as None, Left, Center, or Right. The WordPress subject you're utilizing, nonetheless, might not have these arrangement styles represented in its template. On the off chance that you set the arrangement to Left, for instance, however the picture on your blog doesn't seem, by all accounts, to be adjusted by any means, you may need to add a couple of styles to your subject's template.

You can likewise utilize the WordPress Add an Image window to embed a full photograph display into your posts. Transfer every one of your images; at that point as opposed to tapping the Insert into Post catch, click the Save All Changes catch at the base of the Add an Image window.

4.4 Podcasting and Video Blogging

Many Web website proprietors need to go past simply offering composed substance for the utilization of their guests by offering various sorts of media, including sound and video documents. WordPress makes it entirely simple to incorporate these various kinds of media records in your posts and pages by utilizing the inherent document transfer include. Regardless of whether you're delivering your own recordings for distribution or embedding other individuals' recordings, setting a video document in a blog post has never been simpler with WordPress. The previous advances enable you to embed a hyperlink that your readers can snap to see the video on another Web website, (for example, YouTube). Be that as it may, in the event that you initiate WordPress' clever Auto-Embed include, WordPress can automatically embed a significant number of these recordings inside your posts and pages.

At present, WordPress automatically embeds recordings from YouTube, Vimeo, DailyMotion, blip.tv, Flickr, Hulu, Viddler, Qik, Revision3, Scibd, PhotoBucket, PollDaddy, and Google Videom, just as VideoPress-type recordings from WordPress.tv WordPress doesn't embed a video player in the post, it embeds just a connect to the video; be that as it may, on the off chance that you have the Auto-Embed highlight enacted, WordPress endeavors to embed the video inside a video player. On the off chance that WordPress can't embed a video player, it shows the connection that your guests should click so as to open the video in another window to see it.

Sound documents can be music records or voice accounts, for example, chronicles of you addressing your readers. These records add a pleasant individual touch to your blog. You can without much of a stretch offer sound records on your blog by utilizing the Upload Audio include in WordPress. After you embed a sound document in a blog post, your readers can hear it out on their PCs, or download it onto a MP3 player and hear it out on their drives to work, in the event that they need.

Some incredible WordPress plugins for sound dealing with can improve the usefulness of the record uploader and help you oversee sound documents in your blog posts. In case you're a podcaster and mean to store sound documents on your Web facilitating account, you may need to add expanded capacity and data transfer capacity to your record with the goal that you don't come up short on space or acquire higher charges from your Web facilitating supplier.

On the off chance that you need to see just the records you've transferred, click the Edit connect in the Media menu, found in the left navigation menu of the Dashboard, which opens the Media Library page.

4.5 Custom Fields

A WordPress template contains static bits of information that you can depend on to show up on your site. These static things incorporate components, for example, the title, the substance, the date, etc. Be that as it may, consider the possibility that you need more. Let's assume you compose a week after week book-audit post on your site and need to incorporate a posting of late surveys and going with thumbnails of the books; you can, using Custom Fields, without having to retype the rundown each time you do an audit. You can include truly a large number of auto-organized bits of information like this, (for example, book audits or motion picture surveys, for instance) by including Custom Fields your WordPress blog. You make Custom Fields on a for every post or per-page premise, which implies that you can make a boundless measure of them and add them just to specific posts. They help you make additional information for your posts and pages by utilizing the Custom Fields interface, which is shrouded in the accompanying segment.

Things being what they are, what would you be able to do with Custom Fields? Extremely, the main right answer is: Anything you need. Your creative mind is your possibly limit with regards to the various sorts of information you can add to your posts by utilizing Custom Fields. Custom Fields permit the site proprietor the adaptability of characterizing certain bits of information for each post. To utilize Custom Fields, you do require a touch of learning about how to explore through WordPress subject templates since you need to embed a WordPress capacity tag, with explicit parameters, in the body of the template record.

You can add multiple Custom Fields to one post. To do as such, essentially include the Name and the Value of the Custom Field in the fitting text boxes on the Write Post page, and after that snap the Add Custom Field catch so as to appoint the information to your post. You will do this for every Custom Field you need to add to your post.

Custom Fields are viewed as additional information, separate from the post content itself, for your blog posts, and WordPress alludes to them as metadata. The Custom Field Name and Value get put away in the database in the wp_postmetadata table, which monitors which Names and Values, are relegated to each post. You can locate a Custom Fields module on the Write Page screen in the Dashboard, too; in this way, you can add Custom Fields to either your posts or pages, as required.

You need to include this code for the mind-set Custom Field just one time; after you add the template capacity code to your template for the state of mind Custom Field, you can characterize your present mind-set in each post you publish to your site by utilizing the Custom Fields interface.

4.6 Content Management System

A content management system (CMS) is a system used to make and keep up your whole site. It incorporates apparatuses for publishing and altering, just as for searching and recovering data and content. A CMS gives you a chance to keep up your Web webpage with practically zero learning of HTML. You can make, change, recover, and update your content while never contacting the code required to play out those errands.

Design Portfolio is the name of a classification that she made in the WordPress Dashboard. Rather than utilizing a static page for the showcase of her portfolio, she utilized a class template to deal with the presentation of all presents made on the Design Portfolio classification.

You can make separate sidebar templates for various pages of your site by utilizing a basic incorporate proclamation. When you compose an incorporate explanation, you're basically disclosing to WordPress that you need it to incorporate a particular record on a particular page. You can do multiple things with WordPress to expand it past the blog. The couple of down to earth models in this part utilize the default Twenty Ten subject tell you the best way to utilize

WordPress to make a completely useful Web website that has a CMS stage — anything from the littlest individual webpage to a huge business webpage. The post_class() segment is the coolest piece of the template. This template label advises WordPress to embed explicit HTML markup in your template that enables you to utilize CSS to make custom styles for clingy posts, categories, and labels. By having the post_class() tag in the template, WordPress embeds HTML markup that enables you to utilize CSS to style clingy posts, or presents doled out on explicit labels or categories, with various styling than the remainder of your posts.

A style is made for all posts that have a white foundation with a slight silver outskirt and 10 pixels of cushioning space between the post text and the fringe of the post.

This code makes a style for all posts that have been designated as 'clingy' in the post choices on the Write Post page to show up on your site with a white foundation, a thick red outskirt, and 10 pixels of cushioning space between the post text and fringe of the post. This CSS styles all posts labeled with News with a light dim foundation and a slender dark fringe with 10 pixels of cushioning between the post text and outskirt of the post.

Another component in WordPress (new as of form 3.0) is an element called custom post types. This element permits you, the website proprietor, to make diverse content sorts for your WordPress webpage that give you increasingly innovative command over how various kinds of content are entered, published, and showed on your WordPress Web webpage.

By and by, we wish WordPress had called this element custom content sorts so individuals didn't inaccurately believe that custom post types relate to posts as it were. Custom post types aren't generally the posts that you know as blog posts. Custom post types are an alternate method for overseeing content on your blog, by characterizing what sort of content it is, the means by which it is shown on your webpage, and how it works — however they're not really posts. Custom post types enable you to make new and valuable kinds of content on your Web website, including a brilliant and simple approach to publish those content sorts to your webpage. So as to make and utilize custom post types on your site, you should be sure that your WordPress subject contains the right code and capacities. In the accompanying advances, we make a fundamental custom post type called Generic Content.

After you complete the previous strides to include the Generic Content custom post type to your site, another post type marked Generic shows up in the left navigation menu of the Dashboard.

You can include and publish new content by utilizing the new custom post type, much the same as when you compose and publish blog posts.

Search engine optimization (SEO) is the act of setting up your site to make it as simple as feasible for the significant search engines to creep and store your information in their systems with the goal that your site shows up as high as conceivable in the search returns.

WordPress is prepared to make a domain that is inviting to search engines, giving them simple navigation through your files, categories, and pages. WordPress gives this condition a perfect code base, content that is effectively refreshed through the WordPress interface, and a strong navigation structure. Catchphrases are the initial step on your adventure toward incredible search engine results. Search engines rely upon watchwords, and individuals use catchphrases to search for content. You can display your content such that lets search engines list your website effectively by giving your blog posts and pages titles that bode well and arrange with the real content being exhibited. In case you're doing a post on a specific point, ensure that the title of the post contains at any rate a couple of watchwords about that specific theme. This training gives the search engines significantly more ammo to list your site in searches applicable to the theme of your post. When you compose your posts and pages, and need to ensure that your content shows up in the principal page of search results with the goal that individuals will discover your site, you have to remember those individuals when you're making the content.

At the point when search engines visit your site to slither through your content, they don't perceive how pleasantly you've designed your site. They're searching for words which they're getting to incorporate into their databases. You, the site proprietor, need to ensure that your posts and pages utilize the words and expressions that you need to incorporate into search engines.

In the event that your post is about a formula for singed green tomatoes, for instance, you have to include a watchword or expression that you figure individuals will utilize when they search for the subject. In the event that you figure individuals would utilize the expression formula for singed green tomatoes as a search term, you might need to incorporate that expression in the content and title of your post. Search engines additionally consider your to be as catchphrases that are applicable to the content on your site. Along these lines, ensure that you're giving your categories names that are important to the content you're giving on your site. Making explicit class titles helps search engines, yet in addition enables your readers to find content that is identified with themes they are keen on.

Categories utilize the custom permalink structure, much the same as posts do. Along these lines, links to your WordPress categories additionally become watchword instruments inside your site to help the search engines — and, at last, search engine clients — locate the content.

CHAPTER 5: SEO AND SOCIAL MEDIA

5.1 Content Exposure

A great deal of online merchants suggest that you drive whatever number eyeballs as could be expected under the circumstances to your website by utilizing social-casting a ballot devices and different techniques. In spite of the fact that this system expands your traffic numbers and may incidentally support your certainty, it's a momentary arrangement. The vast majority of your new guests won't have a great deal of enthusiasm for your content and subsequently won't come back to your site. There's a major distinction between a peruser and a guest — readers pursue your blog on a predictable premise, and guests look at your website and after that proceed onward to the following page that catches their eye. Utilize a methodology where you gradually fabricate traffic by focusing on potential readers — not simply guests.

By making great content, making it effectively shareable, and after that partaking inside gatherings of intrigued individuals, you can set up aptitude and assemble a network around your content. A people group is substantially more dominant than a lot of void guests — individuals in a network frequently become promoters and supporters of your blog.

The main mainstay of my every day activity on the Web is content. Despite the fact that the Web has seen a developing shift away from content to network, regardless I accept that content is the best. Networks based around basic interests crash and burn except if they have the content there for individuals to float around. Facebook gatherings, for instance, command due to the abundance of content they offer: the posts, links, recordings, and other media individuals make inside that gathering. Without the content, the gathering wouldn't exist.

Content is the single greatest board in my social-Web reasoning. When I started to blog on MySpace, I had a little after of around 30 individuals. After some time, I saw that the more I composed, the more individuals spread the news about my composition, and I understood that progressively content fundamentally rose to a bigger group of spectators for my work. I analyzed other effective bloggers and found that one of the consistent themes between every one of them was the measure of content that they were putting out — fruitful bloggers would in general post multiple times each week. I concluded that I expected to concentrate on putting out progressively content, and you should, as well.

All these blog components are critical on the social Web. Individuals need to peruse and see data that they find fascinating, that is pleasing, and that is explicit to their needs. Ensure you consider every one of these features of a blog when you make content for your blog.

Correspondence is the second mainstay of my way of thinking about the social Web. While my blog's content developed, I chose to attempt to compose in any event three times each week. The more I composed, the more remarks I'd get. Now and again, I'd get upwards of ten remarks on a blog posting. I could hardly imagine how ten individuals really felt it merited their opportunity to dedicate two or three minutes to answering to what I'd composed. Understanding the social part of the social Web was fundamental to my prosperity. Individuals utilize the social Web as a noteworthy method of correspondence. The correspondence part of my blog and others plays into the by and large online discussion that is going on, a discussion that can begin by an article, which a blogger covers in a blog post about that point, which a peruser remarks on, which prompts someone else to blog a reaction to those remarks or that blog, which gets its own arrangement of remarks. Having a grip on this idea and perceiving how it works not just brings you better accomplishment on the social Web, yet in addition makes you a superior member. Having a methodology by which you just need to take from the social Web leaves you at last fruitless: No issue how incredible your content, you have to have a degree of support and make individuals feel that you're speaking with them, not simply talking at them.

The last mainstay of my hypothesis is the possibility of consistency. When you produce any kind of content that you offer multiple times each week or regularly, individuals start to anticipate consistency. Numerous bloggers don't post reliably, and accordingly, they baffle their readers. In spite of the fact that this desire applies to blogging, when all is said in done, it truly matters on MySpace and other interpersonal organizations where the interconnectivity between the author and the group of spectators arrives at new statures. This applies to authors who have enormous followings on Facebook and Twitter, and who use them as their central matter of contact with their peruser.

At the point when bloggers start to increase some footing inside a network, they start to need to sustain their group of spectators progressively content. At times the content turns out to be intensely watered down on the grounds that they are posting to such an extent. Bloggers frequently start to lose the quality control they have by presenting everything that springs on brain. The nature of the content, what the individuals are there for, rapidly starts to dissolve and you can lose the crowd you have fabricated. By staying with a daily practice and building up consistency in your posting, you let readers comprehend what's in store and you turned into a piece of their daily practice. On the off chance that you instill yourself in somebody's life, the person is going to come back to your blog much of the time and become a supporter for what you're doing.

Go to considerable lengths to guarantee that the quality content you produce doesn't experience the ill effects of blogging all the more regularly. Bloggers frequently profit by a well-known post, increase a group of people, and after that become conflicting with the nature of their content. They either move away from their unique specialty or start to post ill-conceived or set up together blog passages. At the point when their blog quality endures, those bloggers start to lose their group of spectators and never can recuperate. It's simply impractical for each post or bit of content that a blogger thinks of to be high caliber. Additionally, you can only with significant effort judge which presents are going on be effective and which aren't. I've by and by composed posts in five minutes that got a larger number of perspectives and had a superior gathering than posts that I took hours to create. In any case, readers can truly tell when you're calling it in and simply posting for posting. On the off chance that you drive yourself to post for a really long time, the nature of your blog and your consistency can vacate the premises.

Promotion likewise turned into a significant factor while my blog developed. The a lot of the time that I right now spend blogging includes advancing content, not delivering it. When I began blogging on MySpace, I needed to make an everyday practice of advancing my work on a predictable premise, regardless of whether it was for just ten minutes per day. Setting up a daily schedule and getting to be predictable in what I did helped me make a bigger after than a great deal of different bloggers had. A great many people were hesitant to advance their content, which I've constantly thought to be silly. Regardless of how stunning your content is, on the off chance that you don't have a promotional system, no one will ever get some answers concerning it. Probably the best thing about the social Web is that you can share what you find with other individuals. Sharing is such an essential idea. It's such a simple, insightful, and fun activity. You discover content that you like and offer it with your gatherings of companions on the Web, who may discover what you shared accommodating or intriguing and pass it on to their gathering of companions. Be that as it may, a great deal of locales do an exceptionally poor activity of enabling clients to share content. While you set up your WordPress site, consider how you need readers to share your content.

Correspondence is such a significant piece of online life, and correspondence is a two-way road. In online life, correspondence isn't a bullhorn; you have to associate with individuals. In the event that you need the prizes of interest, you have to tune in, just as talk. This thought frequently gets lost when individuals start utilizing web based life to advance their content.

As a blogger, you regularly fill in as the showcasing individual for your own blog. So as to pick up readership, you have to take an interest with your potential crowd in networks where they are as of now partaking. Furthermore, you can truly use taking part in these networks in the event that you comprehend the bloggers in your specialty, work with them to potentially get a visitor blogging space, or even get links from them in their blogrolls.

After you incorporate arrangements of bloggers you might want to target, you can start to separate the rundown and figure out who are the influencers in your specialty, including individuals whom I like to call concealed influencers. Shrouded influencers are individuals that have a huge social engraving that doesn't really appear on their blog. For instance, a few bloggers don't have a ton of analysts on their blog however their Twitter channel is trailed by many thousands.

After you recognize the influencers, you need to pull in them to your blog. In the event that influencers read your blog, they may offer you visitor blogging spots, share your content, and structure an association with you so you can be commonly gainful to one another.

Not exclusively would you be able to get the consideration of a famous blogger by participating in discussion on their blog, you likewise get the consideration of that blogger's readership. In the event that the readers and observers like your commitment, you can get extra traffic, new readers, and even conceivably high rankings back links into your Web webpage; all since you left a remark on the blog.

When you utilize any of the strategies in the previous rundown, the three C's (content, communication, and consistency) become effective. When you speak with these bloggers, you have to ensure that you have predictable content on your webpage. Attempting to contact another blogger when you have just three posts all out doesn't present the most validity yet after you've worked at it for a couple of months, doing blogger effort can furnish you with a decent method to develop your group of spectators.

Despite the fact that apparatuses, for example, Tweetdeck and Hootsuite are better designed for a functioning and vital Twitter nearness, being able to tweet from your WordPress Dashboard enables individuals to refresh all their internet based life from one spot. For individuals simply beginning in online networking, this mix makes your web-based social networking utilize productive and continually reminds you to take part.

Facebook joining is another key procedure to think about when you're setting up your blog just because. To begin with, incorporate the Facebook-sharing element inside your blog, which should be possible with the Share this or add this module. With more than 450 million clients, Facebook is an absolute necessity has sharing alternative for any blog.

5.2 Developing a Social-Media Licensing Hub

A social-media listening center point is an accumulation of data from a few sources, including notices of your blog, catchphrases or themes that you expound on, and even data about contenders.

In any case, the majority of these administrations cost cash and give you somewhere else to sign in to — and you may not utilize this sort of administration to its full capacity. For a private company or an autonomous blogger, the speculation (both time and money related) doesn't generally bode well. By utilizing the intensity of the WordPress stage, you can without much of a stretch cut down on both the time and monetary responsibility of checking stages.

When you start to take part in the realm of social media, one of the most significant things you can do is screen what Internet clients are stating about your organization, your blog, yourself, or your items. By exploring what Internet clients are stating, you can discover and take an interest in exchanges about your blog or organization, and go to a comprehension about the manner in which your locale sees your blog (or organization). With this data, you can take part by reacting to remarks on different blogs, Twitter, or message sheets, or by making focused on content without anyone else blog.

The discussions occurring about your zone of intrigue or specialty add up to extremely extraordinary insight. For a business, paying little heed to whether you take an interest in social media, social-media clients are discussing your organization, so you should know what they're stating. In case you're blogging about a specific point, you can advance your content by following what individuals from your specialty are examining about it.

By checking your specialty you basically can listen stealthily on a huge number of discussions every day, and after that pick and pick the ones where you need to partake. The social-media listening center point you make enables you to pursue different discussions going on through microblogging administrations, for example, Twitter, Facebook, blogs, news locales, message sheets, and even remarks on YouTube. In the event that somebody says something negative regarding you, you can react rapidly to fix the circumstance. You could make endeavors step in and right any deception being said about your business, blog, or zone of intrigue. You could ensure that individuals are educated about what you're doing. This is the advantage of setting up a social-media observing center.

The arrangement in WordPress that we portray in this section gives you the comfort of having everything in one spot and can enable you to screen your image, organization, or blog. The restrictions of the WordPress stage imply that you can screen just five distinct groupings, so you can't utilize this strategy as a swap for an undertaking observing instrument for a huge organization. Furthermore, in the event that you possess an eatery, inn, or bar, and need to get survey destinations, for example, Yelp and Trip Advisor, these devices can't do it.

Some observes instruments get blog inclusion, Twitter comments, and message board remarks. Others get content made around video and pictures. Evaluate these distinctive checking administrations and figure out which give you the best outcomes and which make you feel the most agreeable. At that point pick the best apparatuses to make a decent checking blend. One arrangement most likely can't cover everything, so try different things with various mixes of devices.

Albeit a portion of the checking apparatuses in the accompanying areas don't have any significant bearing to each kind of Web webpage, we would incorporate these devices in most observing arrangements. Before you start bringing the feed into your WordPress Dashboard, you should get the update through email for a couple of days to test out the nature of the outcomes you're getting. Beginning with messages enables you to finetune the catchphrases you use and enables you to test out and limited down what you need to screen. Doing this spares you the hour of parsing all your RSS channels, mixing them all together, and after that returning and alter everything in light of the fact that they are set up wrong. Utilizing the email as a test is an enormous timesaver.

Social Mention is somewhat not the same as the other free devices since it has notion investigation incorporated with its page. Despite the fact that this data doesn't get pulled in by means of RSS channel, regardless you may need to once in a while take a gander at it since it shows the feeling around your site. Opinion score rates content around your site by evaluating it positive, negative, and nonpartisan. Albeit automated supposition score is frequently loose, this gives you a decent broad thought of how your site is seen. Social Mention additionally demonstrates the conclusion scores identified with the search term you entered — the absolute positive notices, unbiased notices, and negative notices. On the off chance that you look down the page, you can see visual charts for the top catchphrases utilized, the top clients covering this region, the top hashtags utilized on Twitter, and the locales that show up most every now and again in your search.

Be cautious about depending too intensely on automated conclusion investigation in both free and paid apparatuses. The innovation doesn't exist right presently to automatically gauge notion with high precision; utilize this examination as a general picture, as opposed to an exact portrayal.

The quality of BackType is in its blog remarks focusing on, so evaluate the search capacity to perceive what it returns. BackType may not be an absolute necessity include device since it is constrained in extension, however on the off chance that individuals online are discussing and referencing your image or blog frequently in blog remarks, you may think that its a commendable source.

At the hour of this composition, BackType is checking just tracks dependent on a particular URL instead of search terms, and has closed down its search engine until it's coordinated into a bigger stage. For instance, in the event that you needed to screen Google you would need to pick Google.com and not the search term Google. We incorporate it since its new stage can conceivably overshadow a portion of different players in this space, so it merits your opportunity to look at.

We order Boardreader as an unquestionable requirement include apparatus since its specialty centers around gatherings and message sheets, where discussions have been going on any longer than just Facebook and Twitter. Numerous other observing instruments frequently neglect these territories when looking at checking the Web, however you can discover such a significant number of energetic networks that merit being a piece of, notwithstanding observing what is being said about your blog or organization.

In the wake of evaluating the different checking administrations, you can make a blend of administrations to bring into your WordPress Dashboard. You import the aftereffects of these checking administrations by utilizing RSS (Really Simple Syndication). You can consolidate distinctive single RSS channels into one RSS channel and make a sorted out arrangement for all the data you need to oversee. For instance in the event that you have different RSS channels from various sources around the watchwords "cookies" you can join them all into one RSS channel. Or then again in the event that you need to join different channels based off sources, similar to all your Twitter RSS channels, you can do that too.

5.3 Understanding Analytics

Each business on the essence of the Earth needs to make sense of what works and what doesn't on the off chance that it needs to succeed. Bloggers frequently know essential measurements about their blogs, for example, the present number on their hit counters or what number of individuals buys in to their blogs. Be that as it may, these details simply give you the comprehensive view, and they don't generally address why something is or isn't working. You have to get in any event an essential comprehension of analytics on the off chance that you need to use your blog without limit. The information given by free projects, for example, Google Analytics can truly enable you to develop as a blogger.

Google Analytics gives you a huge measure of data on your content. The objective of this part is to enable you to translate the information, comprehend where your traffic is coming from, comprehend which of your content is the most mainstream among your guests, realize how to draw relationships between's different informational indexes, and utilize this data to shape the content you compose. This procedure may sound very quirky and bookkeeper like, however in actuality, it gives you a guide that causes you improve your business.

Be that as it may, you should see analytics not as a lot of numbers, yet as an apparatus set that recounts to a story. It can reveal to you how individuals are discovering your content, what content is most prominent, and where clients are sharing that content. Comprehending what kind of content is mainstream, where your site is prevalent (in which time zones, nations and states, for instance), and even what time of day your posts get more readers is all truly important data. Understanding your group of spectators' enthusiasm for your content, just as inclinations for when and how to peruse your content, is significant.

WordPress.com gives a truly decent detail bundle for its facilitated blog clients. Not long after propelling, WordPress.com gave a WordPress Stats module that self-facilitated clients can utilize. In the event that you utilize this bundle, your details show up on the WordPress Dashboard, yet to penetrate down further into them, you have to get to the details on WordPress.com. The upsides of WordPress details are that they are entirely simple to introduce and exhibit an improved diagram of your information. On the drawback, they don't bore as profound as Analytics and the announcing isn't as inside and out. With Analytics you can customize various reports, which you can't do with WordPress details.

The eyes of online business, skip rate addresses the nature of your passage page. The all the more convincing your greeting pages, the more guests remain on your site and convert into buyers, supporters, or whatever activity you need them to finish. You can limit ricochet rates by fitting points of arrival to every advertisement that you run or to the crowd dependent on the alluding. Greeting pages ought to give the data and administrations that the promotion guarantees. A database file passage that recognizes a particular record or archive. Keyword searching is the most widely recognized type of text search on the Web. Most search engines do their text question and recovery by utilizing keywords. Except if the author of the Web record indicates the keywords for their archive, the search engine needs to decide them. Basically, search engines haul out and list words that it decides are huge. A search engine is bound to esteem words significant if those words show up close to the start of a report and are rehashed a few times all through the record.

A referral happens when a client clicks any hyperlink that takes the person in question to a page or record in another Web website; it could be text, a picture, or some other sort of connection. At the point when a client touches base at your site from another site, the server records the referral data in the hit log for each document mentioned by that client. On the off chance that the client found the connection by utilizing a search engine, the server records the search engine's name and any keywords utilized, also. Referrals give you a sign of what social media webpage, just as links from other Web locales and blogs, are guiding traffic to your blog.

Joining the PostRank module with Google Analytics demonstrates to you the numbers identified with how clients view, share, or examine your posts in different social-media outlets and PostRank additionally indicates you explicitly where these dialogs are occurring, which Google Analytics doesn't do. You can utilize this data to make sense of how much your presents need on be shared to get the numbers you're seeing from Twitter, Delicious, and different administrations.

5.4 Search Engine Optimization

Google, Yahoo!, Bing, and other search engines massively affect a blog. Search engines can undoubtedly allude the biggest measure of traffic to your site and, whenever managed appropriately, can enable you to grow a huge crowd in time. Regularly, bloggers don't find the significance of search engine optimization (SEO) until their blogs have been around for some time. By setting aside the effort to ensure that you're following SEO best rehearses as it so happens, you can receive the benefits of a reliable progression of search engine traffic.

Search engine optimization manages following prescribed procedures with regards to blogging. By simply following these straightforward rules and by utilizing WordPress, you can expand search engine traffic to your blog. That is all. To be completely forthright, you presumably won't rank number one in extremely intense categories just by following SEO best rehearses. Be that as it may, you certainly can build your traffic altogether and improve your position for some long-tail keywords. Long-tail keywords will be keywords that aren't searched for frequently, yet when you accumulate positioning for a great deal of them over some undefined time frame, the traffic includes.

Bloggers need whatever number search results as could be allowed on the initial two pages of Google and other search engines to be from their blogs. This search-results point is a more sensible objective than attempting to rank number one for a profoundly focused keyword.

Utilizing WordPress for your blogging stage or content management system, accompanies a few points of interest, including that WordPress was designed to capacity well with search engines. Search engines can slither the source code of a WordPress webpage pretty effectively, which disposes of issues that a great deal of Web software engineers face when streamlining a website.

URLs where your content is for all time housed. While your blog develops and you include more posts, the things on your first page get pushed off the first page of your blog and are supplanted by late content. Guests can without much of a stretch bookmark and offer permalinks so they can come back to that particular post on your blog, so these old posts can live on. One of the specialized advantages of WordPress is that it utilizes the Apache mod_rewrite module to build up the permalink system, which enables you to make and customize your permalink structure.

When you post new content, WordPress has a worked in pinging system that informs major lists automatically with the goal that they can come and creep your site once more. This system enables accelerate the ordering to process and keeps your search results ebb and flow and significant.

Web optimization, social media, and design all go inseparably. You can push a huge amount of individuals to your Web page by utilizing legitimate SEO and powerful social-media profiles, however in the event that your blog has a befuddling or ineffectively done design, guests aren't going to remain. In like manner, an ineffectively designed site keeps a great deal of search engines from perusing your content.

When you start changing your code or adding a ton of plugins to your site, verify whether your code approves. Approved code implies that the code on your Web webpage fits a base standard for programs. Else, you could be averting search engines from effectively slithering your destinations.

Search engines couldn't care less what your site resembles in light of the fact that they can't perceive what your site resembles; their crawlers care just about the content. The slithers care about the material in your blog, the manner in which it's titled, the words you use, and the manner in which you structure them. You have to remember this center when you make the content of your blog. Your URL structure and the keywords, post titles, and images you use in posts all affect how your blog positions. Having an essential comprehension about how search engines see your content can enable you to compose content progressively alluring to search engines.

Search engines investigate the keywords or blend of keywords you use. Keywords are frequently contrasted with the words found inside links managing individuals back to the post and in the title of the post itself to check whether they coordinate. The better these keywords adjust, the better positioning you get from the search engine.

Search engines examine the title of your blog post for keyword content. In case you're focusing on a particular keyword in your post and that keyword is referenced all through the post, notice it in the post title, also. Likewise, the two individuals and search engines place a ton of significant worth on the early expressions of a title.

Perhaps the coolest thing about WordPress is the manner in which it enables you to alter permalinks from inside a post page. You can generally alter the URL to be marginally not quite the same as the automated post title with the goal that it contains pertinent keywords for search terms, particularly on the off chance that you compose an adorable title for the post. On the off chance that content is the best, at that point links are the money that keeps the ruler in influence. Regardless of how great a site you have, how incredible your content, and how well you enhance that content, you need links. Search engines survey the links streaming into your webpage for number and quality, and assess your Web website as needs be.

On the off chance that a top notch site that has a high Google Page Rank highlights a connect to your page, search engines pay heed and accept that you have authority regarding a matter. Search engines consider these excellent links more significant than low-quality links. Be that as it may, having a decent measure of mid-quality links can help, also.

Getting recorded on a blogroll, having a pingback or trackback when a blogger makes reference to your content in their posts, or notwithstanding leaving a remark on somebody's blog can give links once more into your webpage. In the event that you need to look at what number of links you as of now have coming into your site, go to Google and type link:www.yoursite.com into the search text box and snap Google Search. You can likewise search for contender's locales to see where they're recorded and to what destinations they're connected.

This interior and outside connecting methodology utilizes the idea of column posts, in which you have a couple of pages of content that you consider high worth and attempt to manufacture outer and inside links into them with the goal that you can get these posts positioned exceptionally on search results. Despite the fact that presenting your blog to indexes may not be as significant as submitting to search engines, you may even now need to do it. Since rounding out at least 40 structures is quite dreary, make a solitary report wherein you prewrite all the essential data: site title, URL, portrayal, contact data, and your enrollment data. This template enables accelerate the accommodation to procedure to these destinations.

The metadata on a Web webpage contains the data that portrays to search engines what your website is about. Also, the data regularly contained in the metadata appears as the genuine search engine brings about Google. The search engine pulls the page title and page portrayal that show up in search results from the header of your blog. On the off chance that you don't do anything to control this data, Google and other search engines regularly pull their depiction from the page title and the initial couple of sentences of a blog post.

Incorporate unmistakable page titles, depictions, and focused on keywords for each post by means of these plugins or systems: This data affects your outcomes and regularly causes individuals choose to tap the connection to your Web website. You can utilize this data in various ways. For instance, you can perceive what terms you should work into your content. SEMRush gives not just data about what terms search engines use to rank these destinations, yet in addition how aggressive a portion of those keywords are with other sites that are like yours.

You can utilize the general ideas of why WordPress is useful for SEO, the significance of your content, and researching your specialty that we talk about in past areas of this section when you set up your blog, compose key content, and start to incorporate links with your Web webpage.

In case you're not an expert Web designer, presumably you don't do a ton of coding to your webpage. So we don't go indepth on the correct utilization of JavaScript or how best to improve your code. Be that as it may, on the off chance that you make some little alters to your WordPress establishment or include a great deal of code through gadgets, do it appropriately by putting it straightforwardly into your CSS, as opposed to coding into your site. Coding these highlights appropriately improves the speed of your site, how rapidly it burdens, and how search engines slither the site.

Another essential design include regularly neglected when setting up a site, pagination makes base navigation that permits individuals and search engines to explore to different pages. Pagination can truly support the two individuals and search engines explore through your classification pages.

In the event that you have a colossal blogroll, do exclude it on your sidebar all through the webpage.

Truth be told, on the off chance that you need to incorporate something that gigantic, make a page for every one of your links; having them on your sidebar all through the site hinders the speed wherein the pages on your site stacks in your guests program and with all these outbound links, it drains page rank everywhere. Keep in mind: Links pass on authority, when you connect to a site or a site links to you, the connection is stating that your site has an incentive for the keyword in the connection. So assess the links that you have and consider whether you truly need to connection to that Web webpage.

Regularly, when bloggers begin, they pursue each administration under the sun, including Web locales that expect you to put corresponding links or flags on your Web page. Each one of those links and standards rapidly transform your Web website into an awful NASCAR vehicle, and your webpage's exhibition corrupts in light of the fact that it needs to stack every one of those outer codes. Be particular about what you placed into your sidebar.

WordPress has one noteworthy issue with regards to SEO: It makes such a large number of spots for your content to live that copy content can befuddle search engines. Fortunately, plugins and some essential altering effectively fare thee well of these issues.

To begin with, deal with your file page on your site, which is the page that presentations chronicles, for example, class, date-based files, etc. You don't need your file page to present full blog posts, just truncated variants (short selections) of your posts. Check your subject to perceive how your file is displayed. In the event that your chronicle shows total posts, see whether your subject has directions about how to change your file introduction

5.5 Exploring Popular SEO Plugins

You've made it this far, which implies that you have the ideas of SEO down and the beginnings of your methodology appropriately mapped out: Now you have to introduce the instruments. All these plugins have a decent engineer behind them and a decent reputation.

A few plugins in the WordPress module catalog help with SEO, so it's difficult to choose which ones to utilize. In this section, we furnish you with the plugins that are the most widely recognized, and the ones that we use ourselves, since they are a portion of the more-strong and dependable plugins accessible that bring great SEO results. Utilizing the Robots Meta module enables you to control how your site is slithered by the search engines, enabling you to conceal content that you would prefer not to be seen via search engine robots and to guarantee that search engine crawlers see just what you need them to see. It disposes of copy content by keeping crawlers from ordering classification, author, and label pages, just concentrating on your fundamental content. Likewise, this module enables you to effortlessly include the check apparatuses from Yahoo! Webpage Explorer, Bing's Webmaster Central, and Google's Webmaster Tools. In the event that you would prefer not to alter your header, you can without much of a stretch utilize this apparatus to include the different code that these search engines demand you to use to check your Web page.

This module separates every choice on the arrangement page, which enables you to preselect alternatives immediately or roll out certain improvements to the module. We don't separate each alternative inside the module since when you drift over any of the fields, the module gives top to bottom detail on what each field is, alongside useful inline help documentation for you. Be that as it may, we do recommend that you make a couple of changes, from the default settings, directly from the beginning. Despite the fact that you may believe that every one of these URLs are the equivalent; in fact, they're all unique. In the canonicalization procedure, Google picks which one of those URLs best speaks to your site from that gathering. When choosing to utilize standard URLs in the All in One SEO module, you are revealing to Google which URL you need them to pick.

The majority of the rest of the choices that are chosen, as a matter of course, should work fine for your site. Nonetheless, you should choose the Use No Index for Archives and Use No Index for Tag Archives check boxes to ensure that the search engines are not ordering your chronicles pages, which would give the search engines copy content that they have just recorded.

You can utilize the All in One SEO Pack ideal out of the crate, without changing any of the default alternatives that are as of now set for you: If you aren't sure about tweaking it, you don't need to do it. However, remember to place in the best possible data for your landing page on the Options page of the module; this incorporates your landing page title, depiction, and keywords.

You will never need to visit your sitemap, or look after it. The XML Sitemap Generator keeps up the record for you. Each time you publish another post or page on your Web webpage, the module automatically refreshes your sitemap with the data and advises significant search engines, similar to Google, Bing, and Ask.com that you have refreshed your website with new content. Fundamentally, the module sends a solicitation to the search engines to go to your site and list your new content in their search engines.

The various default settings are fine for you to utilize, so leave those in its present condition. In the Sitemap Content area, select the accompanying check boxes: Include Homepage, Include Posts, Include Static Pages, Include Categories, and Include the Last Mortification Time. Making these determinations takes into account your site to get crept by the search engines the most effective way.

The Twenty Ten topic is intended to offer a spotless design style that is exceptionally customizable for the great many WordPress clients who simply need a straightforward search for their site that spotlights on their content. Accordingly, the textual style medications are sharp and simple to peruse. Huge numbers of the new inherent subject highlights enable the client to make basic yet exquisite changes to the topic, including transferring new element images and altering the foundation hues.

Engaging in Reddit, Digg, and other social-bookmarking networks enables you to take an interest in social media with individuals who have comparable interests, and you can incorporate links with your site by submitting content to social-news and bookmarking destinations.

We're not going to remove the enjoyment from blogging by revealing to you that you have to plan out your posts from this point until the part of the bargain. In any case, it doesn't damage to make a rundown of a portion of the keywords that your rivals rank for and a portion of the content they've examined. Take that rundown and apply it to new posts, or compose evergreen content (themes that aren't opportune) revolved around what you need to state. Arranging out your blog can truly help in making sense of what keywords you need to target when you need to compose content to improve for positioning for focused keywords. On the off chance that you feel that your blog is more news-or recent developments arranged, make a reference rundown of keywords to join into your more up to date posts with the goal that you can rank for these focused on terms. In the event that you have an enormous blogroll, do exclude it on your sidebar all through the webpage. Truth be told, in the event that you need to incorporate something that gigantic, make a page for every one of your links; having them on your sidebar all through the site hinders the speed wherein the pages on your site stacks in your guests program and with all these outbound links, it drains page rank everywhere. Keep in mind: Links pass on authority, when you connect to a site or a site links to you, the connection is stating that your site has an incentive for the keyword in the connection. So assess the links that you have and consider whether you truly need to connection to that Web website.

You will never need to visit your sitemap, or look after it. The XML Sitemap Generator keeps up the document for you. Each time you publish another post or page on your Web webpage, the module automatically refreshes your sitemap with the data and informs real search engines, similar to Google, Bing, and Ask.com that you have refreshed your website with new content. Fundamentally, the module sends a solicitation to the search engines to go to your site and file your new content in their search engines. Having a Google Webmaster record is likewise something you can do to further help Google in finding and ordering new content on your webpage. In the event that you don't as of now have one, you can pursue one at Google.com. After you sign in to your Google Account, you can set up the Google Webmaster devices and add your sitemap to Google. The various default settings are fine for you to utilize, so leave those as it stands. In the Sitemap Content area, select the accompanying check boxes: Include Homepage, Include Posts, Include Static Pages, Include Categories, and Include the Last Mortification Time. Making these determinations takes into consideration your site to get crept by the search engines the most effective way.

Yoast Breadcrumbs adds navigation breadcrumbs to your site. Despite the fact that you can introduce and enact the module like some other module, you have to experience a couple of additional means to get the breadcrumbs to appear on your page. For most standard WordPress subjects you have to include the accompanying code into the template where you need the module to show up.

As a matter of course, the footer in the Twenty Ten subject is widgetized so the footer grows to demonstrate any content you add to any of the four gadget prepared zones. At the point when this subject is actuated in the WordPress Widgets board, the gadget prepared regions are marked First Footer Widget Area, Second Footer Widget Area, Third Footer Widget Area, and Fourth Footer Widget Area, as appeared in the topic design from left to right. Later in this part, you find how to apply the footer gadgets to your site. To resize and trim your picture, drag one of the eight boxes situated at the corners and the center of each side of the picture. You can likewise click inside the picture and move the whole picture up or down to get the ideal situation and editing impact that you need.

On the off chance that you transfer an inappropriate picture from your PC or the picture doesn't look the manner in which you trusted, there's an advantageous Remove Background Image catch on the Custom Background page. Utilizing this catch totally expels the picture from the Custom Background settings and enables you to begin once again with an alternate picture.

Navigational menus are essential pieces of your site's design. They advise your site guests where to go and how to get to significant data or territories on your site. The Menus highlight discharged in WordPress 3.0 was a very noteworthy expansion to the effectively incredible programming that permitted more prominent power over the navigational regions.

Like the way the simplified WordPress Widgets highlight empowers clients to change regions of their locales without knowing a great deal of code, the new Menus highlight offers a simple method to mix it up of navigational links to your site, just as make optional menu bars (if your subject offers multiple menu regions).

Moreover, the Menus highlight improved WordPress further by enabling clients to effectively make progressively conventional Web destinations, which some of the time need multiple and more different navigational regions than a normal blog design uses or needs. Twenty Ten accompanies the proper code in the navigation menus that utilize this vigorous component.

After you spare your navigation menu, you can utilize the simplified interface to improve your menu. Furthermore, you can make subpages under top-level menu things by moving menu things somewhat to one side underneath the top-level menu things. Not jumbling up the navigation bar and sorting out content legitimately can be helpful for locales with loads of page content.

You can likewise make multiple custom menus and add them to your topic through gadget zones by utilizing the Custom Menu gadget, navigation zones if your subject backings multiple menu territories, or extra menu zones by embeddings the WordPress template tag straightforwardly into your topic's template documents.

WordPress gadgets are useful instruments worked in to the WordPress.com application. They enable you to organize the presentation of content in your blog sidebar, for example, your blogroll(s), ongoing posts, and month to month and classification file records. With gadgets, mastermind and show the content in the sidebar of your blog without knowing a solitary piece of PHP or HTML. For this situation, Widget territories are the locales in your subject that enable you to embed and orchestrate content, (for example, a rundown of your ongoing blog presents or links on your preferred destinations) or custom menus, by moving (and altering) accessible gadgets (appeared on the WordPress Dashboard's Widget page) into those relating zones. Numerous gadgets offered by WordPress (and those additional occasionally by WordPress topics and plugins) give simplified establishment of further developed capacities typically accessible just in the event that you composed code legitimately into your topic records. Pick Widgets on the Appearance menu in the Dashboard. The Widgets page shows the accessible gadgets. This element is a major draw since it gives you a chance to control what highlights you use and where you place them without knowing a lick of code.

To investigate the Twenty Ten topic's gadget prepared zones, pick Appearance Widgets on the WordPress Dashboard. The Widgets page shows Primary Widget Area, Secondary Widget Area, First Footer Widget Area, Second Footer Widget Area, Third Footer Widget Area, and Fourth Footer Widget Area.

To add gadgets to your sidebar and footer, you simplified gadgets from the Available Widgets segment to the ideal gadget territory. For instance, to add a Search box to the correct sidebar of the default format, drag the Search gadget from the Available Widgets segment to the Primary Widget Area.

The Widgets page records every one of the gadgets that are accessible for your WordPress site. On the correct side of the Widgets page are the sidebar and footer territories designated in your subject. You drag your chose gadget from the Available Widgets segment into your picked gadget territory on the right. To expel a gadget from your sidebar, click the bolt to one side of the gadget title and after that snap the Delete interface. WordPress expels the gadget from the correct side of the page and places it back in the Available Widgets list. On the off chance that you need to evacuate a gadget, yet need WordPress to recall the settings that you arranged for it, rather than tapping the Delete connect, essentially drag the gadget into the Inactive Widget regions on the correct side of the Widgets page, at the base of the page. This stores the gadget and every one of the settings for sometime later.

After you select and design your gadgets, click the Visit Site catch at the highest point of your WordPress Dashboard, and your blog's sidebar coordinates the content (and request of the content) of the Widgets page sidebar. How cool is that? You can return to the Widgets page and improve the things, just as include and evacuate things, however much you might want.

The quantity of choices accessible for altering a gadget relies upon the gadget. Some have various editable choices; others basically let you compose a title for the gadget region. The Recent Posts gadget has two choices: one for altering the title of the gadget and one to decide what number of ongoing presents in plain view.

Made in the USA
Monee, IL
17 December 2019